A Primer on Employment and Wages

The Primer series is under the editorial supervision of
PETER L. BERNSTEIN.

A
PRIMER
ON
EMPLOYMENT
AND
WAGES

Walter Galenson

RANDOM HOUSE

New York

FOR

Emily, Alice, and David

Contents

A Primer on Employment and Wages

Introduction

The American people have cause to congratulate themselves on what their economy achieved during the first half of the current decade. The nation's gross national product, which measures the total output of goods and services, has been rising slightly more than 4 percent a year since 1960. Some 3.7 million more people were at work in 1964 than in 1960, bringing total employment over the 70 million mark for the first time. The average factory worker family of four (where the wife was not working) saw its real weekly earnings, after deducting social security and income taxes, increase from $84 to $92.50 during the four years.* By any conceivable index, the United States is the most prosperous nation in the world, and the character and rate of its economic expansion are contributing to the maintenance of its imposing advantage.

But looming on the horizon are some clouds which temper our optimism for the future. The productivity of our factories and workshops is rising almost twice as rapidly as it did during the 1950's, turning out goods with an

* These figures are both in 1964 prices.

even smaller proportion of labor input. This would be all
to the good were it not for the fact that an unprece-
dentedly large number of young people are knocking at the
factory gates in search of employment. After World War
II, the country went on what can only be described as a
baby binge. In 1947, there were 3.8 million births, compared with only 2.8 million in 1945. These babies are now
reaching working age. If unemployment is not to grow beyond the present level, the economy will have to provide
jobs for at least 1.5 million persons a year during the next
decade, 600,000 a year more than the number added during the prosperous years 1960–1964. Moreover, the new
jobs will have to be at sufficiently high rates of pay to enable the recipients to purchase the automobiles, houses,
and other goods that the economy is capable of producing,
and, indeed, *must* produce if the economic advance is to
continue.

The nice balance of economic forces necessary to provide smooth expansion is not likely to materialize by itself.
Maladjustments in the form of unemployment and poverty
are already all too evident. The average annual rate of unemployment since 1958 has been on a significantly higher
plateau than during the preceding decade. In the midst of
prosperity for the majority, 35 million Americans are living at what the federal government considers to be the
poverty level. An additional 30 million enjoy only very
meager fare, if they are not actually poverty-stricken. Unless appropriate measures are taken to counteract the existing maladjustments, the entire economy may be dragged
down into recession.

To accomplish these objectives without incurring an in-
ordinate amount of price inflation will be a difficult task.
The price level has been remarkably stable since 1957;
some economists believe that the average annual increase
of 1.5 percent in consumer prices since that year has been
largely offset by improvements in the quality of products
sold. A question has been raised about the possibility of

achieving full employment without setting in motion an upward spiral of wage and price movements. Many people believe that unemployment is a necessary cost of maintaining a stable price level. Others reply that if this is true, the cost is too high. There is a more optimistic position which envisions the peaceful coexistence of full employment and price stability, given skillful management of the economy.

It is with this general range of problems that we shall be concerned in the following pages. But the reader will understand that there are no simple solutions, else the great effort that has gone into their study would long ago have borne fruit and yielded final, conclusive answers. This is not to say that no progress has been made. The state of economic knowledge prevailing in the 1920's, which proved helpless to prevent, or even to anticipate, the catastrophe of the Great Depression, seems backward and remote by present standards. Nevertheless, economics is still far from an exact science, and economists continue to grope for more precise tools of policy.

Before embarking upon the more exciting aspects of the subject, it is necessary to set the stage by presenting some factual material, and the early chapters of the book are devoted to this end. We deal first with the complex shifts that have been taking place in our labor force under the impact of changes in the demographic structure of the population, the development of new industries and the decline of old ones, and the rather striking modifications in the psychological attitude of the American people toward gainful employment. Detailed analysis of the labor force and its attributes is relatively new. The *1965 Manpower Report of the President,* which presents an impressive volume of relevant factual material, is the third in what will be an annual series of publications of great value for understanding the economy. Only a few of the manpower highlights are presented in Chapter I, but the reader will find his patience rewarded through a deeper understanding of the phenomena involved.

Chapter II attempts to do the same thing for wages and salaries. It is necessary to know the various wage terms commonly in use, but, even more important, it is essential to gain some appreciation of the marvelously complex system of compensation which makes it possible for a modern industrial society to operate successfully. Many naive solutions to problems are advanced by the less well-informed because of an insufficient understanding of the delicate balance of wage relationships, and of the possible consequences of drastic change.

Chapter III is devoted to trade unionism. Trade unionism might be regarded as a digression, but it is difficult, to my mind, to discuss wages and employment without first touching upon the major institution of the labor market. The functioning of our economic system, and particularly of the labor market, has undergone profound changes since the advent of a powerful labor movement in the 1930's. Not only have the unions added a new dimension to wage-price determination through collective bargaining, but they have also contributed in no small measure to changing public attitudes toward unemployment and poverty. The historical and organizational material set forth in the chapter is necessarily minimal, but the reader may supplement this by looking into some of the books suggested in the Bibliography.

In Chapters IV and V, some theoretical and practical ideas about the relationship between wages and employment are developed. I have endeavored to make the material comprehensible to the newcomer to economics, and anyone who has been exposed to an elementary economics course will immediately recognize some familiar concepts. It is possible to discuss the subject on a more intuitive basis, but even the modest theoretical apparatus introduced simplifies the exposition and enables the reader more readily to grasp the relations among the variables with which we are dealing—wages, prices, employment, and productivity.

The last three chapters deal with what might be described as the pathology of the subject—the failure of the system to generate jobs and affluence for all. Some of the possible reasons for the failure are considered, and the book ends with an analysis of the measures that are now being undertaken by the federal government to improve the operation of the system, together with a few suggestions of what further steps may prove to be necessary.

My main concern has been to raise a question that may well prove to be one of the most crucial of our time: Are unemployment and poverty inevitable under the American capitalist system? My own belief is that they are not, and that our major problem lies not so much in the organization of society as in the attitudes of people toward the responsibility of government for the proper functioning of the economy. This is the principal theme of the book.

Part

I

THE LABOR MARKET

I

The Labor Force

Excess population poses grave economic problems in many of the developing nations at the present time. It is often a major barrier to economic growth. Even in the industrial countries there is some concern with the population explosion. Yet it has never been more apparent that the true wealth of a nation lies in its manpower resources.

The resolution of this apparent paradox lies in the distinction between total population and that portion of it which is usefully and profitably employed. At any given time, a certain proportion of the inhabitants of a country is "economically active," to use a term commonly employed in international statistics. This proportion varies greatly from one country to another, and also over a period of time within a single country. For example, the figure for the United States is currently about 40 percent, while for the Soviet Union it is 48 percent. In the United States, the "participation rate" (the ratio of persons in the labor force to the non-institutional population aged 14 and over, a somewhat different way of expressing the economically active population) reached a postwar peak of 59.3 percent in

1956, but fell to 57.4 percent in 1964. This may not seem like a major fluctuation, but 2 percent of our current labor force comes to 1.5 million people.

Other things being equal, the greater the number and the higher the quality of a nation's labor force, the more likely is that nation to be prosperous. But for this to be true, at least two conditions must be met: the labor force must be employed, and the employment must be productive. A highly developed nation is not likely to prosper in the long run if it permits substantial portions of its manpower resources to remain unemployed, while it will be of little avail to an underdeveloped nation if every man and woman in it is employed at a bare subsistence level. If these conditions can be met, future population growth should hold no terrors.

The basic factors that determine how many people are willing to work at any given time are quite complex. They are bound up with demography, economics, sociology, and psychology. The demographic factors are the easiest to understand. From 1947 to 1964, the population of working age in the United States grew by 26.5 million people, thus greatly enlarging the absolute pool of individuals from which workers can be drawn. Changes in the age and sex composition of the population had an important impact on the employment potential, but in the final analysis, it is the seemingly relentless overall growth that is the most striking aspect of our recent population development.

If the demographic forces were the only ones to be taken into account, the problem of employment planning would be greatly simplified. We cannot predict the birthrate with exactness, but once we know the number of people born, mortality tables enable us to project the population forward with considerable accuracy. The remaining factors that influence the size of the labor force and the participation rate, however, are less stable and more subtle, and are subject to a great deal of forecasting error.

Let us consider first the employment of women, which is perhaps the most startling manpower development since the war. The participation rate of women in the U.S. labor force (*i.e.,* the proportion of women of working age who work or want work) has risen steadily from 31 percent in 1947 to 37.4 percent in 1964. If the 1947 rate had remained unchanged, we would have 4 million fewer women in our labor force than we now have. For the remainder of the current decade, it is estimated that new women workers will enter the labor force at more than double the rate for men, and will constitute almost 35 percent of our 25-year-old-and-over working population by 1970. We will have to find jobs for an additional 2½ million women during the six years 1965–1970.*

The largest increases in participation among women have occurred within the age groups from 35 to 65 years. For one group in particular, 45–54 years, there has been what can only be described as a spectacular rise in the participation rate from 32.7 percent in 1947 to 51.4 percent in 1964. But even among younger women, who might be expected to have small children to care for, and therefore to be fully occupied at home, there has been a remarkable rise in the tendency to accept gainful employment outside the home.

What has caused this revolutionary transformation of the working patterns of the nation's women can only be guessed at. Perhaps the change was set in motion during the war, when many women were drawn into the labor market and entered occupations from which they had been barred previously by tradition. The large-scale unemployment of the 1930's, which made it difficult for married women to hold jobs in many lines of work—school teaching, for example—gave way to a much more favorable employment climate. Retail and other services catering to the homemaker have been expanded and improved, and many

* This and subsequent projections of manpower changes during the current decade are those of the U.S. Department of Labor.

domestic chores have been mechanized, making it easier
for women to keep house while holding down a job. Those
sectors of the economy in which women figure most prom-
inently—education, health, clerical work—have grown
more rapidly than the traditional male preserves.

The fact that women are now getting considerably more
education than in the past must also influence their willingness and ability to enter the labor force. There is a high
correlation between the educational attainments of women
and their labor force participation, as the following figures
for March, 1962 clearly show:

Level of Education		Labor Force Participation Rates (*percent*)
ELEMENTARY:	less than 5 years	20.2
	5–7 years	25.5
	8 years	27.0
HIGH SCHOOL:	1–3 years	32.0
	4 years	35.0
COLLEGE:	1–3 years	34.7
	4 years or more	49.5

SOURCE: *Monthly Labor Review,* February, 1964, p. 153. The
data cover all married women, 18 years of age and over, who live
with their husbands.

Apparently the jobs that educated women can get are
much more attractive than those available to their less-
educated sisters, and exert a pull which is more than just
economic in character.

The relationship between family income and female labor force participation is not as straightforward. A survey
in March, 1963, revealed that in families where the husband earned between $3000 and $5000 a year, 36.9 percent of the wives were working, compared with only 28.1
percent when the income of the husband was over $7000.
This is what one might expect, since there is greater economic pressure on the wife to secure paid employment

when her husband's paycheck is small. The disparity in the ratios was even greater (26.5 percent versus 14.9 percent) when there were small children present. But where there were no children under 18 years, the participation rates of the more and less affluent groups were very close together, and for older women, the wealthier ones even exceeded the poorer ones in their propensity to work.

Tying this in with the previous observations on education, something like the following pattern appears to be emerging. Wealthier, and presumably better-educated, women are less compelled by the force of economic circumstance to take outside work when their children are young than is the case with poorer less-educated women. After seeing children through to a stage of self-reliance, however, the wives of husbands with high incomes are entering, or re-entering, the labor market to a much greater extent than the wives of low-income families. Perhaps the reason is essentially economic—to help pay for a second car, a summer cabin, or for the college education of the children. On the other hand, it may be that we are experiencing profound changes in the role of women in American society, and that the greater desire of women to work is a sociological or psychological phenomenon. Whatever the answer, the end is not in sight. While we are not yet facing the danger of a completely matriarchal society, the notion that a woman's place is in the home has become obsolete.

A second group in the labor force that has been the subject of a great deal of discussion is the nation's youth. During the 1950's, the annual increments of young workers to the labor force were moderate, due to the low birthrates before and during the war and to the spread of educational opportunities. In 1960, the number of workers between the ages of 16 and 24 was almost exactly equal to the comparable figure for 1950. Beginning in 1963, however, the large postwar crop of babies began to enter the labor market. During the four years 1960–1964, the 16–24-year age group within the labor force increased by 1.5 million persons, and the upward trend is continuing. It is estimated that by 1970 there will be about 1.3 million more teenagers and 2.8 million more persons aged 20–24 years in the labor force than in 1964, an average annual increase of almost 700,000 a year for the two age groups combined. As we shall see later, labor force membership and employment are two quite different things; there is no assurance whatever that these very large groups of young workers will be able to find jobs. The participation rates of these groups are not expected to decrease, so that the full impact of the population growth will be felt in the labor market.

Third, there are the older workers. In 1900, persons aged 55 years and over constituted 9.5 percent of the total population of the United States. By the time of the 1960 census, this figure had almost doubled, due to a dramatic increase in lifespan and the cessation of large-scale immigration (the immigrants were generally younger people).

Among men aged 55–64, the labor force participation rate has declined somewhat since 1947, but there was a sharp rise among women from 24 percent in 1947 to 40 percent in 1964. The changes in the 65-year-and-over group have been just as striking: 48 percent of the men were in the labor force in 1947 and only 28 percent in 1964, contrasted with an *increase* in percentage of older women in the labor force from 8 to 10 percent.

Men are leaving the labor force earlier than in the past, but the increased propensity of women to take paid employment has counteracted any trend toward their earlier retirement. For men, the major contributing cause is undoubtedly the greater availability of pension plans and the growing rigidity of a fixed retirement age in both private business and government employment. Older women are obviously finding it easier to secure work in the educational, clerical, and sales occupations, which customarily employ large numbers of females.

The decline in labor force participation among men under 65 is disturbing, since it means that many men with up to a decade of working ability are leaving paid employment, often contrary to their desires. It is even debatable whether involuntary retirement at age 65 is good for the nation and for the individual. Particularly in view of the gradual shift from manual to intellectual work, a great deal of potential productivity is lost, while at the same time people who would be happy to remain in their routines are thrown into a life of retirement for which our work-oriented society has not prepared them. Older men are found in relatively large numbers among such self-employed groups as physicians, dentists, and lawyers, who can work as long as they are physically able.* When providing jobs for younger people is difficult, as it is now increasingly, pressure develops to retire older men and women to make room for the youth. But surely this is a major failure rather than a desirable aspect of our social system, if it is true that the older people are not yet ready for the pasture.

A fourth aspect of labor force participation has to do not with any particular group, but with the short-run fluctuation in the number of people desiring to work, out of a given population. The term "secondary worker" has been applied to the housewife, the teenager, or the semi-retired individual who works intermittently depending upon job opportunities and family circumstances. This not inconsiderable group, perhaps as many as 8–10 million people at the present time, lends considerable flexibility to the labor force. When business is good and the demand for labor

---

* It might be argued that since professional work is more interesting than most other work, manual and clerical workers in particular would retire early even in the absence of fixed retirement policy. On the other hand, it may be easier, financially and intellectually, for professionals to make the adjustment to retirement, so that their remaining in the labor force is indicative of a very strong desire to continue working. The tendency toward the elimination of much dull, repetitive work through technological change should result in diminished desirability of early retirement.

rises, the entrance of secondary workers into the labor market helps prevent the emergence of labor bottlenecks. On the downturn, many of these people apparently leave the labor market and thus help to alleviate the problem of open unemployment. But there is some evidence that many secondary workers, particularly those belonging to low-income families, may actually be marginal regular workers who drop out simply because they feel that there is no likelihood of securing work when there is substantial unemployment.

Seasonal and part-time workers may be part of the secondary labor force, though not necessarily so. About 3 million more people are at work during the summer than in the winter, on the average. Among them are students, farm workers, and housewives. Many of these people are not interested in year-round employment, but they make an important contribution to the economy when they are at work.

More than 10 percent of the labor force consists of individuals voluntarily working on a part-time basis. This group includes 80 percent of all employees 17 years of age and less; and 26 percent of employed men and 42 percent of employed women over 65. Part-time work is particularly prevalent among domestic servants and sales personnel. A real problem in the years ahead will be to provide part-time work opportunities for the large numbers of young people who have to support themselves while attending school. The Higher Education Facilities Act of 1963 and the Economic Opportunity Act of 1964 increased the part-time work assistance available to college and university students, but the program is still quite small relative to need.

A category of workers difficult to classify is the "moonlighters," the men and women who hold down more than one job. A survey conducted in 1962 disclosed that almost 3½ million people, about 5 percent of the entire labor force, had two or more jobs. About 40 percent of the second jobs were in self-employment, and a considerable number of moonlighters were public employees who had no access to overtime work in their regular jobs.

Moonlighting has come in for a good deal of criticism on the ground that no one should have two jobs while others are unemployed. Often, however, moonlighters have skills which the unemployed lack, and perform valuable social functions. For example, with repair services so difficult and expensive to come by, we owe a debt of gratitude to men who are willing to spend evenings and weekends fixing broken household machinery and carrying out home repairs. Dual jobs are often held as a means of easing the transition from one type of employment to another; a man may wish to start his own business on a small scale before taking the plunge of leaving a regular position with a steady income. The only unfortunate aspect of moonlighting is that some people should find themselves obliged to work long hours to attain standards of living which are usually far from affluent.

A few words are in order, finally, about participation rates of men of prime working age. As might be expected, labor force participation of this group is typically quite high, running 97 percent and more. Apart from the physically and mentally handicapped, however, there are some men who have given up the search for employment because their educational attainments and social background appear to disqualify them from all available jobs. This is particularly true of Negroes, whose participation rates run from 2 to 5 percent below those of whites in the same age brackets. This failure to utilize fully the capability of the Negroes is one problem to which we shall return in the final chapter.

The variety of jobs in a modern economy is bewildering. When one stops to think of the tremendous multiplicity of tasks that are performed daily in industry, commerce, education, government, and other sectors of the economy, it seems impossible that the right people with the right skills could ever be found to perform them. Yet somehow a constantly changing stream of manpower is directed to economically meaningful work by the operation of the labor market. Later, we will examine more closely the way in which this market functions. For the moment, we will concentrate on the results yielded by the market in terms of industrial and occupational structure.

One of our most dramatic manpower changes in recent years occurred in the mid-1950's, when for the first time white-collar employees exceeded blue-collar workers in number. Moreover, the former group has continued to grow more rapidly than the latter, so that the employment gap between the two is widening. In 1960, employment in professional, sales, and clerical work exceeded the employment of craftsmen, factory operatives, and laborers by 4.5 million. The difference is expected to rise to 10 million by 1970.

This shift in the pattern of employment is the end result of a number of factors operating independently but in the same direction. An important element is the differential rate of productivity growth among major economic sectors. Since the war, output per man-hour (the measure of productivity most commonly used) has risen by more than 3.5 percent a year in agriculture, mining, and public utilities; by 2.5–3.5 percent in manufacturing and transportation; and by less than 2.5 percent in construction, trade, finance, and other services. The more productivity increases, the less labor is needed to turn out a given volume of goods and services. Employment will fall unless a greater amount of output can be produced and sold. The more rapid the increase in productivity, the more rapid must be the rise in demand if employment is to be maintained.

In mining and agriculture, both industries with large proportions of blue-collar workers, employment has fallen by 33 and 40 percent, respectively, since the war. Here, clearly, production has not increased sufficiently to offset the rapid increases in productivity that have occurred. Manufacturing, in which the great majority of blue-collar jobs are to be found, affords 10 percent more employment now than in 1945 despite a substantial productivity advance, due to the seemingly insatiable desire of the American people for more manufactured goods, and to the requirements of national defense and space exploration.

It is the demand for the output of the service industries, however, which has been growing most rapidly. And it is precisely in these industries that productivity growth has been slowest. Either of these factors would have contributed to increasing white-collar employment. Together, they have led to some spectacular results. Employment in wholesale and retail trade has risen by one-third in the last twenty years, and employment in finance, insurance, and real estate by two-thirds. Among the blue-collar industries, construction alone has seen a 50 percent employment increase in the last two decades, due to a continued building boom and lagging productivity advance.

Government is the largest producer of services in our economy, and government employment has risen particularly rapidly: it has more than doubled since 1947. In 1964, some 7.5 million persons were employed by state and local governments, with another 2.5 million in the federal service (plus 2.7 million in the armed forces). Almost 6 million more people employed in private industry were producing goods and services for various governmental agencies. Thus, 18½ million persons, almost a quarter of our entire labor force, were directly dependent upon the government for employment.

The relative importance of governmental activity was greater for certain groups of persons. About 40 percent of all our scientists and engineers are supported by governmental programs, and the defense cutbacks that took place in 1964 consequently fell most heavily upon them. Governmental employment of educational personnel has risen by 76 percent in the last decade; of health personnel, by 63 percent; of policemen, by 48 percent; and of public welfare workers, by 59 percent. Moreover, the demand continues strong. It has been estimated that between 1964 and 1968, state and local governments will hire one-fifth more employees.

Some see in this expansion of government a threat to private enterprise, and argue that if the taxes necessary to finance this huge employment expansion had been lower, the private sector of the economy would have been able to provide more jobs. However, government employment tends to be labor intensive; that is, the money is spent largely for services. (This is not altogether true, of course, of national defense, but those who are opposed to big government are generally not opposed to adequate defense expenditures.) This means that an outlay by government is likely to yield more employment than an outlay by private enterprise.* Moreover, there is no assurance that the taxes saved would necessarily have been converted into effective demand for privately produced goods and services.

All in all, it is most fortunate that the recent expansion of government employment has occurred. From 1947 to 1957, government at all levels provided about 25 percent of the new jobs while from 1957 to 1962, when the growth of private employment slowed down, the government contribution to the new-job gain reached 40 percent. Government has become a major stabilizing force in our economy, not only by pumping in huge amounts of purchasing power, but even more, by directly providing employment.

The outlook for the foreseeable future is for a continuation of present trends. During the next decade, professional and technical work and service and clerical occupa-

---

* Again, there is the counterargument that private employment may be more productive than government employment in some sense. But this is a matter of philosophical attitude rather than economic fact.

tions will continue to increase most rapidly. Professional and technical employment may increase by as much as 40 percent during this period, clerical employment by 33 percent, sales employment by 25 percent. On the other hand, the demand for semi-skilled industrial workers will probably rise by only 15 percent, while the employment of unskilled workers is not expected to increase at all. Skilled workers will do somewhat better, at 25 percent, while the opportunities for farm work may *fall* as much as 25 percent.

In the non-industrial sector, employment in construction, education, and state and local government will tend to grow most rapidly over the next ten years, while mining and agricultural employment will continue in the doldrums. Manufacturing employment as a whole will expand less than the average increase for the entire labor force, though some individual industries may need substantially more manpower: these include electrical equipment, instruments, rubber and plastics, paper, chemicals, and printing.

The employment forecasts manifest the continuation of a long-run development that set in with the beginning of machine technology. Ever since Great Britain inaugurated the Industrial Revolution two centuries ago, mankind has been constantly engaged in substituting machines for human labor. It has proved easier to do this in the production of goods than of services. But the invention, production, installation, and maintenance of sophisticated equipment requires an army of scientists, designers, engineers, organizers, salesmen, and technicians, replacing the men and women who sat at more primitive machines and performed repetitive tasks. The automated man, made famous years ago by Henry Ford and Charlie Chaplin, has yielded to tape and punched cards.

Although we have not yet approached the saturation point in our demand for physical goods, increased leisure and wealth are shifting demand to such services as education, health, entertainment, vacation, and travel, to say nothing of the repair shops which are struggling against an ever increasing load of broken-down consumer durables. How long this process can go on is an interesting question. Perhaps at some date in the indefinite future we will all be busily engaged in taking in one another's washing, while unmanned machines grind out the material products we need. But that time will not yet have arrived in 1975, for there will still be upward of 30 million blue-collar workers, a somewhat diminished proportion of our working population (one-third as compared with about 37 percent in 1960) but nevertheless of central significance to the economy.

There has been an increasing consensus among those concerned with economic growth and development that the chief obstacle to advance, among the underdeveloped nations, is not so much a lack of capital or physical resources, but rather, deficits of trained manpower due to insufficient investment in education. Studies of American economic history have suggested that education has contributed more than any other single factor to the phenomenal development of this country.

There has been a long and persistent rise in the educational attainments of the American labor force. During the last twenty-five years, not too long a period as these things go, the proportion of workers who have completed four years of high school or more rose from 32 to 54 percent, and by 1975, there should be a further increase to 62 percent. Since 1952, the proportion of college graduates has risen from 8 to 11 percent, and a further rise to 14 percent is expected in the course of the next decade. A college education, once available only to the wealthy few, is now looked upon as a natural thing by other social groups as well.

The entire direction of labor demand emphasizes the increasing importance of education as a qualification for employment. The demand for professionals is growing more rapidly than that for any other occupational group. Teachers, physicians, nurses, scientists, and engineers will be in very short supply for some time to come.* Our corps of managers in industry and commerce has been increasing by leaps and bounds, though future growth is expected to be somewhat more moderate than for professionals. Among blue-collar workers, the skilled trades are very much in demand, despite the lack of buoyancy in manual employment as a whole. Many skilled trades require a formal apprenticeship, and for most, a high-school degree is a minimum qualification. Even experienced skilled journeymen must go back to school to qualify for work in new industries like atomic energy and aerospace.

Job content does not remain stable over time, but generally moves in the direction of increased skill requirements, at all levels. Twenty-five years ago the Ph.D. degree was a relative rarity; today it is a minimum requirement for university teaching. Not so long ago, most physicians were general practitioners, but now it is the exceptional man who does not have specialist credentials. A machinery repairman is no longer a jack-of-all-trades, but a TV specialist who must know a fair amount of electronics technology, or a business-machine serviceman with a good grounding in mathematics. Even the last refuge of the mechanically-minded but educationally shy youth, automobile repair, has been invaded by complicated hydraulic

---

* The shortage of teachers will be particularly acute at the college and university levels. The Office of Education estimates that 600,000 teachers at these levels will be needed by 1975 to take care of increased student enrollment, compared with 350,000 in 1964. The gap to be filled is much greater than this, however, since many currently engaged in teaching will retire or leave the profession. On the supply side, only about 185,000 people will be granted the Ph.D. degree from 1964 to 1975, leaving a tremendous deficit of the most highly trained personnel. There may be a slight improvement in the ratio of physicians to population, but not nearly enough to cope with the increased demand for health services. In the case of dentists and nurses, we may actually experience a deterioration in the supply per capita.

systems, automatic gearshifts, and a bewildering variety of cars, both domestic and foreign, each with its own peculiarities. President Johnson summed up the current situation very well in his *1965 Manpower Report:*

Education has immediate high priority. Many manpower difficulties can be traced to educational deficiencies. Today's and tomorrow's world of work put a premium on capacity for skill development and for redevelopment to meet increasingly frequent changes throughout life. Education is the prime developer of such capacity, as well as of ability to use leisure time enjoyably and to attain a higher level of life generally.

II

The Wage System

The great majority of employed people in our society work for wages or salaries. Some 86 percent of all those employed in the United States during 1964 were in this category; only 14 percent were self-employed or unpaid family workers. If agriculture is left out of the picture, the wage and salaried group increases to 90 percent of employment.

This was not always true of the United States, nor is it true today in many less-developed nations. Slavery, indentured service, peonage, the corvée, and other forms of forced labor prevailed in the past in various parts of the world, and are not completely unknown today as an alternative to the labor contract that is freely entered into. The growing preponderance of wage and salary work is of even more recent origin. Even as short a time ago as 1900, the self-employed in agriculture constituted the largest single segment of the American labor force, and this remains the case in many nations of Africa, Asia, and Latin America. To cite a few examples: of all economically active males in Ghana, only 30 percent are wage and salary earners; the comparable figure is 48 percent for Brazil, 28 percent for

the Philippines, 20 percent for Turkey. Even in some of
the more developed nations of Europe, there are still siz-
able contingents of self-employed: 27 percent of the men
in Sweden, 32 percent in France, and 45 percent in Italy.

We have become so used to the wage system that the
idea seems like a very simple one. People work at occupations of their choice, they are paid, they spend or save, as
the case may be. But the difficulties that many nations are
now having in establishing viable wage systems indicate
that the matter is really much more complicated. We rely
neither on the inertia of tradition nor government fiat to
keep people at their jobs or to move them from factory to
factory or from one city to another. They are induced to
stay or to move by the attractiveness of the wage packet
they are able to command. Moreover, this system allocates
the labor force in more efficient fashion than any other that
has yet been devised. It is interesting to note that the Soviet Union, after experimenting with various other forms
of labor market allocation, has come back to complete reliance on a wage system quite similar to that of the United
States. We must, therefore, examine the structure of the
wage system if we are to begin to understand the nature of
the contemporary concept of employment.

Money wages (we shall use this term to cover salaries as
well)* have risen steadily throughout most of the recent
history of the United States. Declines have taken place
during depression years, particularly during the Great Depression of the 1930's, but for the past thirty years, the
trend has been consistently up. However, the rate of

---

* Wages are different from salaries in that wages are paid for
short stated intervals, such as an hour or a day, and usually vary
with the amount of work done. Salaries ordinarily represent fixed
compensation, regularly paid by the week, month, or year, regardless of the quantity of the work done or amount of time spent at
work. The important point here, however, is that most people in
the United States do work for a monetary reward paid them by an
employer. The housewife is the outstanding exception.

change has been subject to considerable variation. During the decade 1945–1955, when we had two inflationary periods, one immediately after World War II and the other during the Korean War, gross hourly earnings in manufacturing rose by 83 percent, whereas since 1955 the increase has tapered off to the more moderate figure of 37 percent, or about 4 percent a year.*

As every housewife knows, money wages tell only part of the story. If one is interested in the extent to which increases in money wages lead to improvement in the standard of living, changes in the prices of goods and services must also be taken into account. The relevant concept is that of *real wages,* that is, money wages adjusted for price changes. Thus, from 1963 to 1964, gross weekly earnings in manufacturing rose by 3.8 percent, but at the same time, the Consumer Price Index of the U.S. Department of Labor (the best indicator we have of changes in living costs) rose by 1.3 percent, so that in fact the improvement in real living standards between these two years was only about 2.5 percent.†

* Gross hourly earnings are only one of a number of possible wage measures. They represent all earnings received for hours actually worked, including premium pay for overtime, holiday, and late-shift work. Wage *rates,* by contrast, include only basic wage scales stipulated in union or individual agreements, and are not affected by the number of hours worked. They simply represent what a man would earn in one hour at the basic scale. Other available wage indicators are straight-time hourly earnings (average hourly earnings, including piece-rate earnings, apart from overtime and other premium pay), average weekly earnings, net spendable weekly earnings (weekly earnings less social security and income taxes), and average annual earnings. Over long periods these various indicators move along roughly the same path, but there may be sharp divergences in different phases of the business cycle.

† The Consumer Price Index is based upon a survey in which a fixed market basket of goods and services normally purchased by families of city wage earners and clerical workers is priced each month. There has been some controversy over the accuracy with which the index measures cost of living changes. It is doubtful whether the 1.3 percent increase from 1963 to 1964 in fact represented any real increase, or to put it another way, whether there was any decline at all in the purchasing power of the dollar between

As in the case of money wages, there has been a persistent upward trend of real wages in the United States. This has not been true of many other countries, and it may help to explain why American workers have been generally satisfied with collective bargaining as opposed to the more militant labor tactics of socialism or syndicalism found elsewhere. A visible improvement in living standards from year to year contributes greatly to social stability and helps prevent the sense of denial of economic progress that has at times impelled workers in other lands to adopt more drastic alternatives.

Real wages tend to move up less rapidly than money wages in periods of inflation, but on the other hand, they decline more slowly in depression. From 1929 to 1933, gross money hourly earnings in manufacturing fell by 22 percent, compared with a 19 percent drop in real earnings. By comparison, real wages increased by 23 percent from 1945 to 1955 and by 18 percent from 1955 to 1964, compared with the much higher money-wage increases cited above.

The cause of this disparity lies in the greater volatility of prices than wages. Wages are sometimes described as being "sticky" due to the money illusion to which all of us are subject in some degree. We hate to get smaller paychecks even if prices are declining still more rapidly, and by the same token, we receive some satisfaction if our pay goes up even in the face of relatively greater increases in living costs. Trade unions will fight like tigers to resist cuts in contractual wage rates, but are apt to be more gentlemanly in the struggle to keep wages moving up with the price level.

Nations find it unavoidable, at times, to reduce real

---

these two years. The reason is that the index does not make adequate allowance for improvements in the quality of goods, which may have been enough to offset the price increase. It should be added that there are great problems of both a conceptual and statistical nature in allowing for quality change.

wages. A poor harvest, deteriorating terms of trade, natural calamities, war—these and other events may reduce the amount of goods available for consumption. The necessary reduction may be effected by reducing money wages with prices unchanged, or by letting prices rise while money wages remain stable. From some points of view the former alternative might be preferable, but it has been an almost universal experience that the latter is much more palatable politically. Indeed, such is the strength of the money illusion that an even more attractive solution is to let both prices and money wages rise, and then recapture the latter by raising taxes. This may work for a time, but not forever, as many nations have learned to their sorrow. If the price inflation becomes sufficiently rapid and continuous, the illusionary veil is lifted, and workers look to their real pay rather than the money wage.*

Wages are but one dimension of compensation for work. Increasingly, other types of income have been supplementing direct wage payments, in the form of fringe benefits paid by employers or by government. The U.S. Department of Commerce estimates that such supplements have risen from 1 percent of wages and salaries in 1929 to 8.2 percent in 1963. The first big increase came during the 1930's with the introduction of federal social-security programs. This was followed after the war by a push on the

---

* There have been a great many interesting episodes since the war that illustrate these points. In some countries, for example, collective agreements provided for automatic wage increases if the cost of living rose, in order to maintain real wages intact. Where the consumer price indexes included sales and other excise taxes, attempts by the governments to reduce consumption through higher taxes were frustrated, since raising the tax rates simply caused an increase in the price index and in wages. To accomplish their objectives, the governments had to get the trade unions to agree that higher taxes could be excluded from the computation of the consumer price index. Unions were willing to acquiesce in this policy only when convinced of its absolute necessity; but they never could have been prevailed upon to permit money wages to be reduced, since few of the leaders could have survived the storm of membership protest that would have followed.

collective-bargaining front, and we now have a variety of health and welfare, pension, and supplementary unemployment-benefit schemes. The U.S. Chamber of Commerce claims that these figures understate the true extent of fringe benefits, and that when paid rest and lunch periods, vacations, and pay for other time not worked are added, the supplement to the average employer's payroll in 1963 was on the order of 28 percent. The two figures can be partly reconciled by taking into account the fact that the Chamber of Commerce includes reduced working time as a fringe benefit, while the Commerce Department does not. If this element is eliminated, the Chamber's figure becomes just double that of the Department. Whichever is the more nearly correct, there is no doubt that this type of income has grown relative to wages. Its attractiveness to the recipient is enhanced by the fact that some fringe benefits are not subject to income tax immediately, or are taxed at lower rates than wages and salaries.

Differences in wages and salaries among individuals, occupations, industries, and localities can be considered most conveniently under two main heads: external, and internal wage structure. By external wage structure we mean the various types of differentials that transcend the single enterprise in scope, while internal differentials are generally limited to those prevailing within a firm. The distinction is sometimes difficult to maintain. For example, regional wage differentials which are external may become internal if we are concerned with wage differences among scattered plants of the same company. Nevertheless, the categories are useful for purposes of exposition.

Wages and salaries are far from uniform throughout the United States. Generally speaking, they are highest on the West Coast and lowest in the Southeast. The basis of the differences has been the subject of considerable debate. Here are some of the factors alleged to account for the

differences: Southern labor may be less efficient than North-
ern, there is a surplus of labor and a dearth of capital
in the South, living costs are lower in the South, and the
weakness of Southern unionism contributes to a lower bargaining power for labor there. These assertions are difficult
to prove, though one or more may be relevant. It is clear,
however, that the South has more than its share of low-
wage industries, while the West Coast, with its electronic
and aerospace complex, is strong in high-wage industries,
so that what appears to be a regional wage difference may
in fact be due largely to industrial differentials.

Regional differentials have been narrowing over the long
pull, but many contrary short-run examples could be cited.
Texas, for example, has gained considerably on New York
since the war, but hardly at all on California, perhaps because Texas and California have had more than their share
of the new defense and space industries. Many states have
done far less well than these two, in effect widening some
interstate differentials in the postwar period.

Similar observations might be made about local labor
markets, with the additional consideration that substantial
differences in living costs between large and small cities
are apt to be reflected in wages.* The same modest annual
living standard budget was priced at $5370 in Houston
and $6567 in Chicago in 1959. However, living costs are
not perfectly correlated with community size as evidenced
by the fact that the same budget would have cost only
$5970 in New York, whereas Seattle was almost on a par
with Chicago.

It is well-established that some industries pay well and
others pay poorly. In terms of hourly earnings (though not
always on an annual basis because of short-time work)
workers in coal mining, construction, automobiles, iron

* A local labor market is a geographical area within which labor
can move fairly freely in terms of the possibility of daily commuting and other factors. It is generally centered about a metropolitan area and includes contiguous suburbs in which some of the
people who work in the city live.

and steel, printing and publishing, and petroleum do better than those in textiles, clothing, retail trade, hotels, and laundries. Moreover, the differences are rather stable over time. The industries which paid relatively high wages in 1890 continue, with a few exceptions, to do so at the present time. Nor does there seem to have been much compression of the structure in terms of percentage wage differences among industries.

Once again, it is easier to state the facts than to explain them. An industry which requires a high level of skill will normally have to pay higher wages than one in which the majority of employees are semi-skilled operatives. High profit margins, lack of competition, a low ratio of labor to total cost, or a low proportion of women may also contribute to an above-average wage level.* But no single factor will necessarily produce this result. Coal mining and construction, both high-wage industries, have high labor-cost ratios, the well-paying petroleum industry is often highly competitive, and the tobacco industry is highly profitable but pays low wages. It may be that if proper weights could be assigned to all the relevant factors, a comprehensive explanation of industrial wage differentials would emerge.

Another type of external wage comparison that can be made is between different firms in the same industry. One might expect to find wage differentials when the firms are scattered geographically, though the extent of the differential may depend on the degree of competition: where firms sell products nationally in direct competition with one another, as in the case of automobiles, there is much less scope for local wage variation than in such local market industries as newspaper publishing or baking. What is puzzling, however, is that even within local labor markets, firms in the same industry pay different wage rates, often substantially different.

---

* All of these may contribute to higher productivity in one industry than another. The relationship between wages and productivity will be considered in Chapter V.

Several ideas may be advanced in explanation. The most plausible is that the high-wage firms want to attract the best qualified and most stable workers, while those at the bottom are willing or have to make do with a poorer quality of labor. A variant of the argument is that profitable firms which are able to pay more do so in order to foster a favorable climate of work, which in turn raises productivity and partly offsets the higher wage cost. It is also true sometimes that firms which are classified in the same industry are really in non-competing subdivisions; for example, a deluxe hotel would have quite different labor requirements from a cheap one located in the same city. To some extent, too, lack of accurate and complete information on the part of workers and employers contributes to the persistence of differentials among firms. This is less likely to be the case in unionized trades, for unions and employer associations are good sources of local wage information.

Occupational wage differentials, which are both external and internal as we have defined these terms, have been declining over the long run. A careful study of the period 1907–1947 resulted in the finding that skilled workers earned twice as much as unskilled workers at the beginning of the period but only half again as much by the end, with the greatest compression taking place in wartime and in the immediate postwar years. Quite recently, however, this trend has slowed down, and may even have been reversed.

It seems logical that people with more skill should earn more than the less skilled, but there is no adequate explanation for the precise differences that prevail. It has been argued that at early stages of economic development a large premium for skill results from an urgent need for skilled personnel in the face of a short supply, as well as from the necessity to induce young people to acquire skills through training. As the economy matures and educational opportunity broadens, the supply of skilled workers increases and at the same time the number of those who are

A Primer on Employment & Wages

willing to perform unskilled work declines, bringing about a better balance in supply and demand, and with it a diminution of the wage differential. Thus, at a time in our history when illiteracy was common, the mere ability to read and write was an asset that could be converted into a cash wage, but now that literacy is almost universal, mere clerical ability no longer pays off. The equalizing tendency may be reinforced by the dilution of skills through mechanization. Some of the highly skilled crafts of yesterday—glass-bottle blowing, railroad telegraphy—are almost extinct, while many others are on their way out.*

Another factor peculiar to the United States may be cited, the sharp reduction in immigration after 1914, cutting off the flow of predominantly unskilled labor, and thus contributing to its higher remuneration. The recent problem of Mexican bracero labor in the United States is very much in point, for the possibility of securing cheap labor from abroad has held down the wages of American agricultural workers. Now that bracero labor will no longer be available, a relative increase in the remuneration of agricultural labor may be anticipated.

This line of argument has much to commend it, but facts may be cited which cast some doubt on its adequacy as a universal theory of occupational differentials. Many contemporary underdeveloped nations have fairly narrow occupational wage differentials, and even where they are wide, the cause may be based on race or religion rather than on the skill component.† The Soviet Union, less de-

---

* However, new crafts are constantly being created, and it would probably not be correct to say that as a nation, we are becoming less differentiated according to skill. The locomotive engineer is being replaced by the airplane pilot, but it could hardly be argued that the latter is a relatively less skilled worker. Some extremely specialized jobs have developed during the past two decades. The only issue is whether all work is being upgraded to the extent that the average difference between unskilled and skilled work is greater or less today than it was twenty-five or fifty years ago. We shall return to this issue later on.

† I do not want to leave the impression that demand and supply

veloped than the United States and with an entirely different industrial history, has skill differentials which do not differ greatly from ours—and both are higher than in most nations of Western Europe. Political and social elements quite obviously impinge upon the purely economic forces to produce the income differentials that various societies find acceptable. How else could one account for the fact that American physicians are relatively much better off than their colleagues in Great Britain or Scandinavia, despite the fact that they are neither better trained nor in shorter supply?

In using the term "internal wage structure," we refer to the network of wage and salary rates paid to employees of a single enterprise. This network cannot be completely independent of the external market. The standards for wage differentials accepted outside the firm must be reflected in what is considered appropriate within the firm as well. If a company departs too markedly from external labor market relationships, it will find itself losing, or unable to hire, certain categories of labor. On the other hand, linkage with the outside world is not rigid. Most firms are somewhat insulated by the reluctance of people to change employment, and wage variation among firms is common, in structure as well as level.

A wage structure grows with a firm, and the hand of the past can never be completely eradicated. At one time, foremen had a considerable amount of latitude in fixing wages on an individual basis, and though this is rarely the case now, many wage relationships established rather haphazardly for this and other reasons have become embedded in the wage structure. These relationships are re-

---

of labor do not influence wages in underdeveloped countries. The point is, however, that tradition, psychology, and social institutions may prove stronger than demand and supply, particularly where the wage system is not fully developed.

flected in men's attitudes and beliefs, which of all things
are the most difficult to change.

As a means of rationalizing internal wage structure, a
practice known as job evaluation has been growing in pop-
ularity. The term is a general one covering a great many
different schemes, but what they all boil down to is a comprehensive effort to rate jobs in terms of such factors as
responsibility, training, physical effort, working conditions,
and safety and health features; to assign numerical weights
to each factor; and to fix compensation on the basis of the
total number of points thus determined for each job.

The proponents of job evaluation, particularly the con-
sulting firms which specialize in installing the various systems, advertise it as scientific and objective, and far supe-
rior to traditional methods of wage determination. But
these claims are greatly exaggerated. It is the essence of
the scientific method that experiments or observations can
be reproduced by different people with identical results,
and this is not the case with job evaluation. At every step
of the way in the process of evaluating jobs, subjective
judgments must be made: in selecting the factors by which
the jobs are to be rated; in assigning weights to them (how
much for responsibility, how much for physical effort?); in
the money-wage rates to be assigned to factor totals.

The great merit of job evaluation lies not in these doubtful claims to scientific accuracy but in the fact that it forces
management to describe and classify jobs with some care,
and to think through the relationships among them. In the
process, anomalies are brought to light and can be corrected.

Trade unions vary in their attitudes toward job evaluation. Some of them look upon it as a management tool
designed to remove wages from collective bargaining, and
either oppose its introduction or offer grudging co-operation
at best. However, increasingly the unions have been willing
to accept job evaluation on condition that they have some
voice in its administration. An outstanding example is the

United Steelworkers of America, which joined in 1947 with all the major firms in the steel industry in a co-operative wage survey that led eventually to a uniform internal wage structure throughout the industry. The union reserved the right to question job evaluations which led to wage rates seemingly out of line with past practice or current expectations, and adjustments were made to prevent inequities. It is interesting to note that Holland evaluated its internal wage structure on a national basis after the war, and that in 1956, the Soviet Union embraced this capitalist invention and has since applied it on a widespread scale.

An issue that arises constantly, not only in job evaluation, but in a much broader context within internal wage systems, is that of equity versus the market. Suppose that a certain job has traditionally been at the top of the promotion ladder, and is normally filled by older, experienced men on the basis of seniority. A technological change now occurs, demanding a new skill which the older employees do not have. In terms of experience, responsibility, and even training, the new job would rate lower than the old one on the evaluation scale. But there may be a scarcity of men possessing the new skill, and in order to find employees, the firm may find itself obliged to rate it above the old ones.

The obvious question is: What about equity for the older men who see their earnings and status subordinated to those of the newcomers? To adjust all wages upward might involve a financial burden beyond the firm's capacity; but to make no adjustment at all might shatter the morale of the older employees. The usual policy is to hedge by giving everyone some increase, no matter how small, in the hope that this will ease the psychological shock. This is easier to do when prices and wages are moving up than when they are stable, since the pain of being surpassed may be eased by the swelling of the pay envelope.

Some would argue that equity is a moral imperative, and should be given heavy weight regardless of economic considerations. But as long as people are motivated to work primarily by what they can earn, and are able to move freely from one job to another, in other words, as long as we continue to operate under a modern system of wages, an internal wage structure cannot depart too radically from market relationships and at the same time perform the function of getting work done in an efficient manner. Where costs and profits are not major considerations, as in the case of churches, philanthropic, and other non-profit organizations, the scope of equity can be broad. But in most situations, it can serve only to temper the harsh judgment of the market.

The wage profile of a firm depends not only upon basic rates, which are the focus of job evaluation, but also upon other types of payment which may result in substantial differences between wage rates and actual earnings. This is true even more for management than for the working force. Bonuses and stock-option schemes can render hazardous direct comparison of executive salaries among firms.

It used to be that when a man was offered a job, a wage rate was quoted which gave him a good idea of what he was likely to take home each week. Now his real compensation depends on a number of elements which would require the services of a skilled actuary to evaluate accurately. Comparing jobs becomes a very sophisticated process, and the proper assessment of net advantages and disadvantages is increasingly difficult to make. This may become an important factor in making people more cautious when it comes to changing jobs.

Wage earners are paid on the basis of time or piecework, or some combination of the two. Time work is simple and unambiguous, but it does not take into account effort or productivity during the unit of time for which payment is made. Piecework relates earnings directly to output, and in theory, at least, provides an incentive for raising production.

In fact, the line between these two wage systems is not clear-cut. Often there is a customary hourly or daily stint, and workers will not exceed that amount regardless of how they are paid. If they are on the low side, the foreman will urge them along, while on the other hand, the man at the next bench will help to restrain "rate-busting" proclivities on the part of colleagues eager for extra money. It is true that earnings of pieceworkers have been higher, historically, than those of day workers, since it is generally believed that pieceworkers put forth more effort. But the two types of earnings must move up and down together, or else workers would shift to the one which was gaining.

Piecework is most practicable where the unit of output is clearly identifiable with an individual or a group, where quantity is more important than quality, and where technological change is not too rapid. The last factor is of particular importance. Once the time-study engineer has determined standard tasks, and the wage per unit has been negotiated with the union, it becomes difficult to persuade workers to permit rates to be changed downward. New machinery or altered methods may augment productivity, but to the worker it would appear that he was being asked to turn out more goods for the same pay. In the past, many employers have taken advantage of the lack of worker bargaining power to cut rates even in the absence of technological change (the hated speedup); the tradition of resisting rate reductions persists.

American industry has used piecework less than most other nations. About 30 percent of all manufacturing workers are paid on this basis, whereas abroad the proportion is usually much higher. In the Soviet Union, the piecework percentage is about 70 percent. The reason for this heavy reliance on piecework, which runs against the communist ideology of "from each according to his abilities and to each according to his needs," was the necessity of getting a good day's work out of millions of raw recruits to industry, drawn from agriculture and not accustomed to the working tempo of the factory. American industrial development was slower, and it was possible to build up socially accepted norms of a fair day's work which provide a working pace that is the envy of the world.*

Methods of wage payment are not unrelated to economic stability. It is easier to keep wages from rising if wages are paid on a time basis. When labor is in short supply, an employer can make upward wage adjustments readily by permitting piece rates to become loose, while raising time rates may expose him to pressure from government or from other employers. Piecework is a major factor in so-called "wage drift," the phenomenon whereby earnings rise above collectively contracted wage rates.

With acceleration of technological change, and particularly the advent of automation, individual piece rates have been giving way to group incentive schemes, and even to plant-wide incentive systems. One of the most publicized is the Kaiser Steel Corporation plan, in which 32.5 percent of saving in labor and material costs is distributed to the participating workers in the form of monthly bonuses. This is quite different from older profit-sharing plans, for the Kaiser workers may be entitled to a bonus even when there are no profits, and conversely, should profits rise due to an increase in product price, it does not follow that any bonus will be paid. The incentive is to reduce costs, over which the workers have some control, rather than to maximize profits, which depend on many factors beyond their control.

---

* This does not mean that American workers necessarily expend more physical effort than their counterparts abroad. The reverse is probably true, due to the greater mechanization of American industry. But there is less idle time and more required attention to the job in American factories than in most other countries. Productivity teams from Great Britain and elsewhere have commented on this, and foreign trainees here have complained about it.

Incentive pay is by no means confined to blue-collar workers, as the widespread use of salary bonuses and stock options for top management testifies. Many white-collar workers, including commission salesmen and self-employed professionals, are compensated on an incentive basis. The growing size of most of our economic organizations, resulting in a divorcement of the individual employee from the observable result of his work, will make the problem of incentives a more crucial one in the years ahead.

This brief review of the trends, structure, and practices that characterize our wage system leaves a great many questions unanswered, but it will serve as an introduction to a complicated subject. The wage system has many faults. There are obvious inequities and irrational vestigial remains which cannot be explained on the basis of current needs. But it has the virtue of being deeply rooted in custom and of having achieved general acceptance. Anyone who does not think this is important has only to study the contemporary experience of underdeveloped nations who are struggling to create systems of compensation which will further their economic growth. Our methods of wage and salary payment are by no means perfect. They are constantly being changed, usually in the direction of greater efficiency. With all its drawbacks, however, the wage system does seem well-adjusted to the economic needs of the nation, and it is unlikely to undergo rapid or drastic modification.

III

The Role of Trade Unions

Trade unions occupy a central position in the American labor market. This is not true in many other countries, where unions are weak and have little power to affect the pattern of wages and employment. But an attempt to analyze how wages and employment are determined in our economy without reference to the labor movement is like listening to a string quartet with the first violin missing; one might get some idea of how the music sounded, but it would be neither interesting nor a reasonable facsimile of the real thing. It is possible, of course, to discuss some of the theoretical aspects of wages and employment in a vacuum. Models can be constructed and manipulated, statistical time series can be correlated, and wide-ranging generalizations can be derived. They are not likely to be of any great use for policy purposes, however, nor to lead to an understanding of real-world phenomena, unless they are anchored firmly in an institutional setting.

It is manifestly impossible, in a work of this size, to cover in any detail the history, structure, government, and policies of American trade unions.* There are hundreds of volumes on library shelves dealing with these matters. All that is attempted here is a quick look at some of the aspects of trade unionism which are of central concern to the main topic of this volume, wages and employment.

The modern history of the American labor movement dates from 1886, when the American Federation of Labor was founded, with Samuel Gompers at its helm. The AFL has been challenged on several occasions, but it always emerged as the mainstream of organized labor in the United States. It has obviously been well-adapted to the American scene.

When the AFL was organized, another labor federation, the Noble Order of the Knights of Labor, had already been in existence for almost two decades. In contrast to the basic principle of organization based on skilled crafts as advocated by Gompers, the Knights stressed geographical locality as the main structural unit, that is, all workers in a city, regardless of trade, were to be affiliated with a single central body, which in turn became part of a national federation of city centrals. In the contest between the two structural forms, craft unionism proved more durable than general-locality unionism. After a meteoric rise in 1885 and 1886, Knights of Labor membership declined with equal speed, and within a few years the organization became defunct.

The AFL weathered bitter employer antagonism and economic crisis to attain the respectable total of 2 million members on the eve of the First World War. It faced some opposition during this early period from a radical movement, the Industrial Workers of the World, which was dedicated to the overthrow of capitalism and its replacement by worker ownership of factories. The IWW (its members were called "Wobblies") was based in the West, and its supporters were mainly the migratory laborers who

* The interested reader is referred to the Bibliography for reference material on labor history.

manned the lumber camps, the docks, and the wheat and cotton fields along the Pacific Coast. These men believed in direct action, not collective bargaining. The strike and sabotage were their favorite weapons, and they expected that one day they would bring capitalism tumbling down by a mammoth general strike. The demise of their ideology, sometimes termed anarcho-syndicalism, was hastened by IWW efforts to impede American participation in the war. Some IWW leaders were imprisoned, others were lynched, and the organization went into eclipse. The basic cause of the decline, however, was the whittling away of its constituency by the growth of a more stable pattern of employment in the West.

The AFL, in contrast to the IWW, co-operated with the federal government and took advantage of the strong demand for labor to boost its membership to 4 million by 1920. But postwar recession and a concerted anti-labor campaign mounted by employers dealt it a heavy blow. On the eve of the Great Depression, AFL membership had fallen below 3 million, and many of its affiliates were completely demoralized.

Depressions are not good times for unions. Unemployed workers, or workers fearing the loss of their jobs or eager to steal the other fellow's, are not union material. The Great Depression, in which unemployment reached the fantastic level of 25 percent of the labor force, was no exception in this respect. An already weak labor movement declined still further. Apart from building construction and the railroads, the economy was largely on an open-shop basis. Labor's future had never looked as bleak. Yet within a few years, new and unprecedented heights were reached.

The key to this dramatic shift in the fortunes of organized labor was political in large measure. Franklin D. Roosevelt was elected to the presidency in 1932 with little support from the trade unions, though most unorganized workers voted for him, but he transformed the attitude of the federal government from one of scarcely disguised hostility to the aspirations of unionism to one of friendliness. A few years later, Congress enacted the National Labor Relations Act, called the Wagner Act, which for the first time provided governmental protection for the right of workers to unionize free from interference, restraint, or coercion by their employers.

The Wagner Act created the National Labor Relations Board, an independent federal agency vested with authority to enforce its provisions. Employers who continued to use such traditional anti-union weapons as labor espionage, blacklisting of active unionists, discharge for union activity, and company unionism, were obliged to mend their ways by Board order, enforceable in the federal courts. Moreover, they were bound by law to engage in collective bargaining with the duly designated representatives of their employees. The Wagner Act ban on employer unfair labor practices was supplemented, in 1947, by a number of union unfair labor practices contained in the Taft-Hartley Act, including the use of secondary boycotts, jurisdictional strikes, and the closed shop. These two pieces of legislation now provide the basic framework for collective bargaining in the United States. The National Labor Relations Board has no authority to settle labor disputes, but it acts as a referee to prevent both labor and management from hitting below the belt.

A very important provision of the Wagner Act which was put in largely at the insistence of the AFL was that providing for majority rule in collective bargaining. This is not the rule in most countries; in Great Britain, for example, an auto plant often has several unions representing workers in a single department, each union speaking for its members only. Under American practice, however, there can be only one bargaining representative in each bargaining unit (though it is possible to have more than one unit within a single plant). Exclusive bargaining rights are vested in that organization which the National Labor Relations Board determines by a secret ballot, or by some other means, has the support of a majority of the workers in the bargaining unit. Adoption of this practice has greatly simplified the collective bargaining process; American employers are not constantly faced with competing labor unions, each one striving to augment its membership by outdoing the others. A great deal of the turmoil that often exists in British, French, and Italian enterprises is due to the prevalence there of proportional representation rather than majority rule as the basic principle of labor representation.

The dominant group in control of the AFL when the Wagner Act was passed, the craft unionists, were more interested in organizing their fellow craftsmen than in the army of semi-skilled workers in the automobile factories, the steel mills, and the other central bastions of mass production in American industry. John L. Lewis, president of the United Mine Workers of America, an old union which had practiced from its start industrial rather than craft organization of coal mines, led a revolt against the unwillingness of the AFL to concede industrial union structure to the mass production workers. He formed the Committee for Industrial Organization (which became later the Congress of Industrial Organizations) in 1935, and mounted flamboyant campaigns in steel, autos, electrical manufacturing, rubber, textiles, and other industries, using mass picketing, the sitdown strike, and other tactics which are now associated with the civil-rights movement. As in the case of civil rights, the American public sympathized with the objectives of the workers, and in spite of the patently illegal aspects of many of the weapons employed, the outcome proved successful. Some employers tried to fight back, and for a time the Little Steel companies and the Ford Motor Company held the CIO at bay, but eventually they went down under the combined pressure of the unions and the federal government, plus the militance of the workers themselves.* The AFL, stung by the unexpected

* It has been said of the French worker that he is willing to die

success of the CIO, intensified its organizing efforts, and soon began to outdistance its rival.

During the Second World War, union strength continued to increase, but the wave of strikes that followed the war intensified a trend of public opinion against unionism which had begun at the close of the 1930's. The result was enactment of the Taft-Hartley Act over a presidential veto and an intense campaign by the unions to stigmatize it as a "slave-labor act." Despite these gloomy forebodings, when the AFL and the CIO reconciled their differences and merged in 1955, their combined membership had reached an all-time high of 16.9 million.

Future prospects seemed favorable. The labor movement was finally united, and costly internecine warfare was largely at an end. The unions had ample financial resources, they had gained social respectability, and few employers were willing to waste time and money in the useless quest for the open shop. Nevertheless, union membership subsequently remained on a plateau, and has even begun to show signs of decline.

The causes are to be sought in a combination of political and economic circumstances. A string of witnesses was paraded before the McClellan investigating committee of the U.S. Senate and revealed a picture of corruption and undemocratic procedure in half a dozen national unions which badly tarnished the public image of the entire labor movement. Combined with this, and more important, the structure of employment was turning against the unions. As we have already seen in Chapter I, white-collar employment grew rapidly, while blue-collar employment stag-

---

on the barricades, but not to pay his union dues. American workers have both paid their dues and demonstrated a capacity to fight hard for what they regarded as their rights. But it is a fortunate aspect of American industrial relations that once a strike is over, people go back to work without rancor, and do not continue to regard their employers as class enemies as so often happens elsewhere. Friendly relationships between employer and employees usually prevail—until the next strike.

nated. The professional, clerical, and sales employees were never attracted by the traditional aims and slogans of manual-worker unions, and allegations of racketeering and corruption confirmed their prejudices.

Try as they might, the unions have had little success in organizing these growing groups. Apart from Southern cotton textiles and small shops, blue-collar employment was largely unionized already, so there was not much room to expand in that direction. And automation began to make inroads into such union strongholds as automobile and steel manufacturing, reducing the union constituency in these well-organized sectors.

Further trade-union growth depends largely on the ability of the unions to appeal to white-collar groups. It is by no means impossible to organize white-collar workers. In Sweden, for example, they have achieved virtually complete unionization, though in an independent federation rather than as part of the traditional blue-collar labor movement. Some AFL–CIO unions in the field, notably in retail trade and government employment, are making good progress. In the meantime, however, it would be a mistake to underestimate the economic power of a movement numbering 17 million persons, comprising 30 percent of the non-agricultural labor force. The unions are well-financed and ably staffed. They have considerable influence at federal, state, and local levels. Their role in the operation of the labor market is central and widely accepted. Their present base is a strong one from which to mount an offensive when the appropriate time comes.

The basic structural unit in labor organizations is the local union, which may cover a single plant or all or part of a community, and can vary in size from a handful to tens of thousands of members. There are about 80,000 local unions in the United States, and it is their stability and soundness which make the American labor movement so strong.

There is great variation among local unions in their freedom to formulate bargaining strategy and to make independent economic decisions. A great deal depends on the industry in which they function. Where production is mainly for a local market, as in the case of construction, the local union is apt to have a good deal of autonomy, since its policies will not have a major impact on allied local unions in other cities. But if a local union is operating in an industry which distributes its products widely, the necessity for co-ordination on a regional or national level becomes apparent. It would not do for every local union in the steel industry to decide on its own wage policies; some locals might put their employers out of business, while others might be persuaded to give their employers a competitive advantage by agreeing to relatively low wages.

Many unions have intermediate bodies standing between the locals and the national organization. These bodies go under different names—district councils, joint boards, conferences—but their rationale is the same: to co-ordinate local union bargaining when either the product market or the labor market dictates uniform policy. The history of the Teamsters Union provides a good example of the response of union structure to an economic need. When trucking was largely an urban industry, local in character, a local union within a city could manage its own affairs without affecting similar locals in other cities. But when over-the-road trucking developed into a major industry, co-ordination of labor conditions among cities serviced by the same trucks became essential. The result was the regional conference (the Western Conference of Teamsters was the first), which gradually assumed more responsibility for making wage and employment decisions.

The next step up the structural ladder brings us to the national union, which has become the real locus of power in the labor movement.* The national union charters lo-

* Some national unions use the term "international" in their titles because they have members in Canada.

cals, and exercises the degree of supervision and control specified in the national constitution. Most union funds are held at the national level, tending further to consolidate national authority. There are some 180 national unions in the United States, about 135 affiliated with the AFL–CIO, the rest independent. They vary in size from the giant Teamsters Union and United Automobile Workers, each with over 1 million members, to small organizations like the Hosiery Workers, the Marble Polishers, the Railroad Yardmasters and the Stove Mounters, which are smaller than many locals in the large industrial unions.

All national unions have one thing in common regardless of size, autonomy. They are bound only by the terms of their own constitutions, elect their own officers, and run their own affairs as they see fit. No other union body can dictate wage or employment policy to them. Affiliation with a federation of national unions like the AFL–CIO is voluntary, and many national organizations have operated successfully as independents. The Teamsters and the United Mine Workers are good current examples. The former was expelled from the AFL–CIO on charges of corruption, while the latter has been on its own for more than two decades because its doughty ex-president, John L. Lewis, was not able to get on with his former colleagues in the AFL and CIO. Another flourishing independent, the International Longshoremen's and Warehousemen's Union, resigned from the CIO when threatened with expulsion for alleged communist domination.

Dues are collected at the local level and the major share is turned over to the national union. The amount of dues varies a good deal among unions, depending upon the earnings of the members and the union welfare benefits afforded. Dues can run from hundreds of dollars a year for airline pilots or licensed deck officers to less than $50 a year for low-paid industrial workers.

At the apex of the union world is the American Federation of Labor–Congress of Industrial Organizations (AFL–

CIO). This organization is very much in the public eye, but its powers and functions are in reality quite limited. It is largely a public-relations and lobbying body, at national and state levels. The AFL–CIO also performs certain co-ordinating functions, and tries to minimize wasteful juris-dictional controversies among its affiliated unions. But it does *not* engage in collective bargaining, it does *not* enter into collective agreements, nor does it call strikes. These are the exclusive provinces of the national unions. The AFL–CIO is financed by a per capita fee paid by its affili-ates, and it has no central fund of its own, normally spend-ing each year just what it takes in.

The only coercive power which the AFL–CIO can exer-cise with respect to its affiliates is expulsion, and this is obviously a weapon to be used with extreme caution. When the Teamsters Union was expelled, the AFL–CIO lost a good portion of its annual income plus the influence represented by almost 1.5 million workers in strategic em-ployment, without any discernible effect on the Teamsters Union. The history and philosophy of the AFL–CIO strongly dispose it against expulsions, and only intense public pressures generated by charges of corruption and communism have led to this drastic expedient.

The details of trade-union government were aired pub-licly in the McClellan Committee hearings already referred to, and several unsavory practices were revealed. One was the disfranchisement of members by putting local unions in trusteeship, a device whereby the local was run by the na-tional union without any local-membership participation whatever. Some union officials were found to have con-fused union funds with their own bank accounts, and others were using their union positions to help make per-sonal business enterprises profitable. The large majority of unions were not involved in these practices, but enough were to convince Congress that government regulation was in order.

The result was the Labor-Management Reporting and

Disclosure Act of 1959, called the Landrum-Griffin Act, and whether because of this law or because of the adverse publicity, unions seem now to be run more honestly and democratically than in the past. In the event of allegedly dishonest elections, the results may be appealed to the Department of Labor and eventually to the federal courts.* There must be full disclosure to the Labor Department of union finances as well as the personal finances of union officials. In fact, a higher degree of moral probity is now required by law of union officers than of the business community.

While the recent improvements in union government are highly desirable, they have had their costs. One of the reasons for lack of democracy in union affairs is the employers' preference to deal with "realistic" leaders rather than with the unruly rank and file. Union officials are specialists in the economics of the labor market, and are in a better position to appraise market possibilities than the man at the bench, and the spur of higher income is not as sharp.† In the past, union officers could generally count on lifetime tenure, unless some cataclysm overtook the union, so that they could afford to take the long view. The Landrum-Griffin Act facilitates opposition to incumbent officials, and is making them more responsive to rank-and-file demands. The opposition can make irresponsible prom-

---

* A dramatic example occurred in the 1965 election for national officers in the International Union of Electrical Workers. The incumbent, James Carey, was declared re-elected, whereupon his challenger appealed the election to the Secretary of Labor, who found that the votes had not been counted correctly and that Carey had lost. The Secretary would probably have asked the federal courts to set aside the election if Carey had not resigned.

† The level of compensation received by union officials is sometimes exaggerated. Very few unions pay salaries of more than $50,000 a year, and more national union presidents earn under than over $20,000. Walter Reuther, with one of the most responsible jobs in labor, earned $24,000 in 1963. Not only do innumerable corporate executives earn more than this, but a great many professionals are above this level. Local union officials generally earn well under $20,000.

ises, and the officers who are saddled with responsibility for collective bargaining may find themselves obliged to counter with demands which they are fully aware cannot be realized. The result may well be more strikes or imprudent wage movements.

There is a real dilemma here. We want unions to be more democratic and responsive to the will of their membership; anything less is inconsistent with our political ideals. We also want them to be economically responsible lest they trigger inflation and instability. The long-run answer is to educate union members about the realities of economic life so that they refrain from demanding too much of their leaders. In the meantime, we must be willing to accept the inconvenience of strikes and the occasional irrationality of wage and other demands as the price of democracy.

It is one of the basic assumptions of economic theory that businessmen are motivated primarily by the quest for maximum profit. This may not be true for all firms at all times. Some economists believe, for example, that enterprises merely seek satisfactory rather than maximum profits in the interest of corporate survival, and that a desire for size or power may also influence business decisions. But the profit maximization assumption has great simplicity and explanatory power, and it has not been supplanted by any other general hypothesis.

What trade unions are aiming at is much more difficult to define. One might say, by analogy, that their goal is the maximization of wages. But this immediately raises complications: Maximum wages for whom? for all present members of the union? for present and potential members? for all employees, regardless of membership, whom the union represents in collective bargaining? Any one of these alternatives, and others that are conceivable, would yield different policies. For example, if the union were concerned only with the welfare of members of long standing, and was operating under a strict seniority system in employment, it might seek a very high level of wages which resulted in unemployment for all except the senior inner circle. If, on the other hand, the goal were employment for as many people as possible, a lower wage level might be permitted. If unemployment benefits to displaced workers were taken into account, there might be still another wage solution.

Political factors of a non-monetary nature are of greater importance in the union than in the business firm. Union officials must stand for re-election periodically, and their economic performance may be relevant to their chances of victory. However, it is more difficult to measure their performance than in the case of corporate executives. Trade unions publish no profit-and-loss statements, and there is no simple measure of success or failure. A bit less in wages can be offset by gains in fringe benefits. It almost never happens that unions seek exactly the same economic package, and this makes the comparison of results among unions a complicated affair. Over a long period, workers may realize that they are losing ground relative to other industries, but year-to-year variations are not normally detected.

Under the circumstances, union leaders may take the line of least resistance in the quiet life: just enough improvement in wages to allay potential membership discontent, but not seeking that extra measure which could be obtained only at some risk of strikes. The follow-the-leader principle operates as well: to do as well, or preferably a bit better, than the nearest similar union is a safe and satisfactory policy.

Samuel Gompers once said that the ultimate goal of American trade unionism was "more—always more." This is not a bad place from which to begin in describing union policy; but unfortunately Gompers never defined what he meant by "more." The crucial question that every employer who begins a collective bargaining session with a union would like to have answered is: What does "more" mean this year in terms of exact cents per hour, pensions, medical insurance, and the like? No one has worked out a satisfactory method of prediction, but a few observations germane to the subject matter of this volume may be made.

The first is that union leaders and their wage committees generally formulate demands against a background of considerable knowledge of the labor and product markets in which they operate. They are aware of the connections between wages and employment, that too ambitious a wage policy may mean some unemployment for their members. They follow price trends for the commodities which their employers sell, as well as profit margins. They do not want to put anyone out of business.* This is not to say that unions never make mistakes in assessing what industry can afford to pay; but it is true that American unions act in a responsible fashion, since they feel that they have a stake in the existing economic system and have no desire to change it radically, much less to destroy it.

Second, union negotiators are generally well aware of the state of the economy, and of their place in it. In recent years, much more than in the past, unions have come to understand that there is a direct relationship between their wage actions and the economic welfare of the nation. The size of the union is relevant here, of course. Where a small organization might reasonably believe that its policies have little impact on the total economy, a large union cannot take this point of view. If they are to act in a responsible fashion, union leaders must, and usually do, give more than passing attention to what the government and the public, as well as their own members, expect of them.

---

* However, most trade unions will have no compunctions about firms which can remain in business only by paying substandard wages. In some cases, unions have sent in their efficiency engineers in attempts to help such firms before letting them go under. But in the final analysis, unions will rarely bail out a firm by permitting it to pay below the union scale. Even if they wanted to do so, other employers would not let them.

Finally, the image of the union leader pushed into extreme and unwise demands by an exigent rank and file has little basis in reality. If the union is doing a reasonably good job in keeping wages moving up, the leadership has a good deal of leeway. Internal pressures can be generated or curbed through control of the union press, meetings, and other means of communication. The serious advancement of a demand that the leadership deems unwise is symptomatic of a breakdown of authority and is unusual.

This does not provide a really satisfactory answer to the issue raised at the outset: How do unions make decisions? But it may serve as an antidote to a view, all too commonly held, of the union leader as an irresponsible, power-hungry demagogue, pursuing his goals without regard for the interests of others, and forcing employers to bend the knee by threatening to bring their operations to a halt. Trade-union leaders tend to be fairly conservative in their economic and political philosophy, and their strong preference is for bargaining rather than the use of force. As in every bargaining situation, agreement cannot always be reached, but the aim, except under very unusual circumstances, is the achievement of a solution which will guarantee union members reasonable wages and steady employment in a healthy economy.

The contemporary collective agreement contains a great variety of provisions in addition to money-wage rates. Most of these relate to the content and the control of jobs. Unions have gradually reduced the area in which management can make unilateral decisions involving conditions of employment. Management policy in hiring, training, layoff and discharge, promotion, work scheduling and assignment, subcontracting, technological change, and discipline are all subject in some degree to the bargaining process. Agreements are growing longer and more complicated. Many management officials are bitter about this trend and have been fighting a rear-guard action against union encroachment on their prerogatives. Nevertheless, the union advance continues, spurred by the desire of workers to have a greater say about the conditions under which they perform their jobs. The quest for democracy at the shop level is as old as the factory system; in a real sense it has gone as far in the United States as anywhere in the world.

Fringe benefits are among the most widely publicized aspects of collective bargaining, apart from wages. Prior to the Great Depression, the AFL was cool to government intervention in labor affairs, and preferred straight money wages to employer welfare schemes. This philosophy was laid to rest by the traumatic events of the Depression, and the labor movement has ever since been one of the warmest supporters of the welfare state. Moreover, it has pioneered the extension of welfare schemes through the power of collective bargaining. Federal old-age insurance is supplemented by a network of private plans which now embrace more than 20 million persons. Supplements to unemployment benefits (sometimes called the guaranteed annual wage) are much more restricted in coverage, but in several industries, such as steel and automobiles, they are widespread. Medical insurance in some form is now enjoyed by most wage earners.

Within the factory, unions have obliged employers to adopt personnel policies which strongly affect the distribution of available employment. Before the days of the union, when an employer had to lay men off, he usually did it on the basis of efficiency. Younger and stronger men were preferred to those whose physical capacities were fading.

Under union conditions, some form of work sharing may be required before any layoffs can be made. This may take the form of a reduction in hours worked, rotation of jobs, prohibition of overtime, or limitations on subcontracting of work. Work-sharing arrangements are most common in seasonal industries, where the extent of the slack work can be predicted with reasonable accuracy. The development of improved unemployment benefit plans has reduced somewhat the urgency of work sharing, since layoffs no longer mean economic catastrophe for the workers affected.

When a layoff becomes necessary for economic reasons, the rule stipulated in most collective agreements is strict seniority: the last to be hired is the first to be fired. Nothing will produce a grievance more quickly than failure to follow the seniority roster—and not only for layoffs, but for promotion as well. If an employer wants to promote a man out of turn, the burden of proof is on him to demonstrate that this is absolutely essential to the efficient operation of the plant. In layoffs, he has virtually no discretion.

The effect of seniority, which is practiced more rigidly in the United States than almost anywhere else in the world, is to enhance the job security of older workers and concentrate unemployment on the younger. The equity of this arrangement may be questioned. Younger men often have heavier family responsibilities and are less able to afford spells of unemployment. On the other hand, they are more flexible and mobile, and find it easier to get new jobs. Whatever the rights and wrongs, trade unions, like most social institutions, are controlled by older people, and they are not likely to reverse this policy.

It is a common assumption that seniority and efficiency are antithetical, and that the application of a strict criterion of merit would better promote operating efficiency. Upon closer examination, however, this may not prove to be true from the standpoint of social policy, however appealing the individual employer may find it. Suppose an older man is discharged from a job and a younger, more able one is kept on. The discharged employee will find it more difficult to adjust to a new job, if he can find one. Since his remaining working life is shorter, the investment in retraining him, whether borne by a private employer or by the government, will have a smaller payoff. His morale will be affected, and he is likely to be less productive in his new job.

The younger man who was retained will perform more efficiently, but he is less attached to the firm and will be more prone to move if he finds a better position. Substantial hiring costs will be entailed in his replacement. The performance of the older people who were kept on must also be taken into account. They may be spurred to increased effort by the fear of layoff, or on the other hand, they may become demoralized.

Whether merit or seniority will yield a net advantage socially or to the individual firm cannot be determined by *a priori* reasoning. The calculation will depend on the degree of merit sacrificed, the supply of labor which the firm can count on, the morale imparted by job security, and above all, the extent of the unemployment prevailing in the labor market. The only point of these comments is to warn against the facile assumption that merit is always necessarily the best policy.

Most unions are open in the sense that they are willing to accept as members anyone hired by the employer. However, seniority, plus the requirement that laid-off workers be rehired before new men are taken on, may effectively close a union where employment opportunities are not expanding. There are craft unions, particularly in the building and printing trades, which limit membership in order to reserve available work for a specific group. This can often be accomplished by the regulation of apprenticeship. (The medical profession, though not unionized in a formal sense, does the same thing by limiting entry into medical schools and through strict licensing procedures.) Until recently, Negroes and other minority groups were barred from membership in several national unions; while all discrimination under union constitutions has now been removed, some local unions still discriminate on a *de facto* basis.

By and large, however, unions are interested in job control rather than in being exclusive, and this is reflected in the heat engendered by the issue of union security agreements. Under a union-shop agreement, all workers are required to become union members in order to keep their jobs.* This strengthens the bargaining power of the union by eliminating non-union workers who might refuse to obey a strike call. There is no intention of limiting employment. Size of membership is a strong plus factor for a union. The prestige and authority of the leadership, as well as financial resources, increase with size.

As of the present writing, nineteen states have so-called right-to-work laws on their books. The effect of such legislation is to outlaw union-shop agreements. In these states, unions must devote more time to organizational work, and there is some evidence that they are more aggressive, particularly in handling plant grievances, in order to keep the membership convinced that they are doing a good job. It is also likely that these laws keep union membership down. At least the unions believe this, to judge by their dislike of right-to-work legislation.

Working rules have been brought to public consciousness under the invidious rubric of featherbedding. Who does not know of the extra man on the diesel train, the printer who sets type which is destroyed without being used (bogus work), the standby musicians who play during intermission when a name band comes to town, the flight engineer on an airplane built to dispense with his services? This list could be expanded, but the problem runs much deeper in fact. The difficulty is that in no industry is there an absolute standard that can be applied in defining a fair day's work. Even within the same trade or occupation, and allowing for differences in technology, daily output is subject to great variation among nations, and even among the different regions of the United States.

---

* This is to be distinguished from the *closed* shop, in which the employer agrees *to hire* only union men. The closed shop is illegal under the Taft-Hartley Act, but it may be legal in intrastate commerce where state law permits.

Work rules are part of the effort to define the working day. They change slowly, even in the absence of unions. When the employer calls for a higher work tempo, he may be told that what he proposes will be injurious to health or safety. There is always the lurking fear on the part of workers that employment opportunities will be reduced. This rather primitive notion, sometimes called the "lump-of-labor" theory, that there is only a fixed amount of work to be done at a particular time, does not make economic sense, but it is a widely held belief nonetheless.*

Under union conditions, working rules become part of the collective agreement. Formal action is required to change them, which may be more difficult than in the case of informal rules in non-union situations. This is what management usually means when it talks about the inflexibility of unions. Even national unions have discovered that disregard of such "local conditions" as the length and number of coffee breaks can endanger otherwise acceptable agreements.

The employment aspects of working rules emerge most clearly in declining industries. It is no accident that featherbedding is most common where employment opportunities are being reduced. Concessions in working rules are easiest to obtain where they can be offset by increased compensation and greater security of employment.

A mixture of several elements is involved in the determination of rules of work: encrusted tradition, ethical notions about the working day, physical and mental stress, employment effects of change. It is easy to condemn inefficient ways of doing things, but efficiency is a relative matter. In the case of Great Britain, it has been asserted frequently, and with some justification, that outmoded work practices add a sufficient amount to the cost of production

* If this theory were true, we could not have technological progress without creating unemployment in proportion to the reduction of labor time per unit of product. The theory neglects, among other things, the increased demand for cheaper products resulting from reduced labor costs.

to hamper Britain's ability to compete in world markets, and change is clearly in order.

The situation is different in the United States. Our products are competitive, and old working rules as such do not add much to costs. Efficiency could certainly be raised; there is hardly a job that could not be done more quickly and effectively through added effort and attention. But whether this would add to the pleasures of life is another matter. We are constantly making choices between goods and leisure, between more automobiles and more coffee breaks. A more relaxed attitude toward the speed of work might be preferable to a shorter work week. There may even be something to be said for the payment of an outright subsidy to an employer to enable him to keep on the job a man who is no longer able to put in a full day's work at top speed because of a decline in his physical or mental faculties. This might be cheaper in the long run than paying unemployment or welfare benefits.

All of this adds up to the conclusion that work rules do not lend themselves to simple legislative regulation. The Taft-Hartley Act contains a prohibition against featherbedding, but it has never been applied. When rules become too costly, enough pressure eventually will be generated to secure their abolition. But this is not to say that radical changes in job content should be made at the whim of the industrial engineer. The changes may reduce production costs, but there are costs to the employees to be taken into account as well. It may be necessary to compensate them for leisure foregone, for increased effort and responsibility, or for the loss of job satisfactions. Collective bargaining is the mechanism through which compensation is assured, and if we become impatient at times with its slow operation, it is well to remember that more authoritarian solutions are apt to be less satisfactory in the long run.

The ultimate weapon of a union to back up its bargaining demands is the strike. The incidence of strikes has declined rather markedly since the war, but this is no solace when a strike does take place, and public inconvenience or danger to economic stability results. For some years now, it has become customary for firms to stockpile steel in advance of strike deadlines, causing sharp fluctuations in production. When strikes threaten, editorials denouncing this "outmoded" method of resolving disputes begin to appear in the newspapers. Suggestions are made for some form of compulsory arbitration if the parties cannot reach a peaceful settlement. However, when the strike is over, nothing much is done beyond the introduction of procedures designed to keep the parties talking longer.

There is a good reason for failure to go further. It lies in the key role of the strike in our system of wage determination. Collective bargaining is the method we rely upon for attaining suitable wage-price relationships, and bargaining implies the possibility of refusing to agree if minimum demands are not met. A refusal to agree carries such penalties as loss of wages and possible loss of jobs for workers, and loss of profits for the employer. The bargaining system is policed by these penalties, for each side knows that extreme demands can only be gained at considerable sacrifice; it thus tends toward moderation. If a particular objective is strongly desired, either by labor or management, there will be a greater willingness to pay the price of a strike or lockout. And the chances are that these objectives will be more justified economically than demands which are advanced without much steam behind them.*

Suppose that a law were enacted banning strikes and lockouts and providing for final settlement of labor disputes by government arbitration boards. Realistic bargaining is not likely to take place under these circumstances.

---

* This is not always true, of course. Inefficient work practices which have become traditional are sometimes defended by unions to the bitter end. But it is more likely that wage demands which are strongly backed are more equitable and economic than those which are put forward for bargaining purposes and are withdrawn in preference to a strike.

Unions could make extreme demands, secure in the knowledge that they would not have to back the demands by recourse to work stoppages. Employers would tend to offer few concessions, knowing that arbitration boards are prone to split the difference and wanting to keep their end of the bargain as low as possible. Each arbitration board would have to be supplied with a wage guide based upon some combination of past wage relationships, productivity, the ethical desirability of greater equality (or inequality) among groups of workers, or the ability of the individual employer to pay. Although all of these criteria enter into collective bargaining, any one of them would be seriously deficient if applied too rigidly. Moreover, if the government, through the wage boards, were to limit workers in their wage demands, the latter, with considerable justice, might demand that profits be similarly controlled.

Collective bargaining backed by strike or lockout does not provide a guarantee that the outcome will be optimum in some economic sense. If there is a preponderance of power on either side—a powerful union facing small employers, a large corporation whose workers are poorly organized—true bargaining cannot take place. Special protection is needed for groups of workers with limited bargaining power, hence our minimum-wage laws. Combinations of strong unions and monopolistic employers may seek their mutual advantage in exploiting the rest of the community.

While collective bargaining is more consonant with our present system of economic organization than administrative wage determination, this does not imply that government must always remain neutral, and let labor and management fight it out on the picket line or reach any agreement that suits their purposes. There may be occasions on which the potential damage of a work stoppage is sufficient to justify government intervention, regardless of other considerations. The railroads seem to be a case in point; the economic consequences of closing them down are such that strike action has been virtually barred. As a result, however, collective bargaining has been severely impaired in terms of its ability to lead to settlement, and the railroads have become a kind of public utility in which both wages and prices are regulated.

In any event, there can be little objection to government mediation. Most labor negotiations end in agreement without a work stoppage, and a good mediator may help find an acceptable solution more quickly. Strike-delaying provisions, such as those contained in the Taft-Hartley Act, may be useful in preventing precipitate action desired by neither party. In the final analysis, however, nothing is better calculated to produce agreement than the realization that there is a deadline beyond which demands must be supported at the cost of income, profits, or even one's job.

Part

II

THE DETERMINATION OF WAGES AND EMPLOYMENT

IV

The Supply and Demand

of Labor to the Firm

In attempting to put together the elements which determine precisely what levels of wages and employment will prevail at any particular time, we must enter the realm of theory. The function of theory is not so much to enable us to describe relationships among phenomena, for this can be done without theory, as, for example, when we examined the trend of wages over time. Its purpose, rather, is to give us an understanding of causation so that we can understand the past and predict the future.

Suppose that we have observed that there was a systematic relationship in the past between the movement of wages and employment. Are we justified in asserting that this relationship will continue into the future, that we can count on employment to respond in a certain way to wage change? Probably not, if all we have to go on is the past relationship, since there may have been changes in the economic environment which might have had the effect of disrupting the relationship. However, if we have a theory explaining the past events, we can examine the present situation to determine whether on theoretical grounds enough has happened to the economy to invalidate the basis of the relationship, or whether in fact the underlying causal factors are still operating.

Before beginning the subject, we must admit at once that wage-employment theory is not in too satisfactory a state. A number of different theories have been advanced in the past, but apart from the one that we shall consider, they have fallen into disuse. In the last ten years the advance in electronic-computer technology has resulted in great changes in the methods of economic research, and we should not be too surprised if new theories were to emerge. At present, however, the marginal-productivity theory of wages is the only one with any substantial support among economists. For all its shortcomings, it provides many insights into the relationships which govern the market, and it is a useful framework within which to marshal the mass of statistical data that is being collected.

The concepts of supply and demand in the market for goods are known to everyone. A large supply and a small demand generally result in falling prices, and vice versa. The same concepts are carried over into the labor market, but the analogy is not perfect because labor has certain characteristics that differentiate it from goods.

There is no single labor market, even within the same community, but rather a whole series of interlocking markets based upon industry, occupation, skill, unionization, and other factors. The labor markets for blue-collar and white-collar workers are quite dissimilar and mostly independent of one another.

Let us conceive, for the moment, of a labor market abstracted from any particular type of labor, and ask what determines its supply. In a fundamental sense, it is the growth or decline in population. We have already noted, however, that in the shorter run, the proportion of the population willing to work varies with economic and social circumstances. In general, it appears that higher wages will tend to raise the rate of labor-force participation.

This is by no means always true. After a certain level of income has been reached, a husband's income may be high enough to discourage his wife from working. His children will remain in school longer. There may be less incentive to work overtime or to moonlight. People may retire earlier and take longer vacations. The events of the past two decades suggest that longer schooling and vacations, and earlier retirement, are the principal negative effects of affluence on the labor supply. More women are working than ever before, while moonlighting and overtime continue to be popular.

If we consider now the position of the individual firm, it can either hire from the pool of locally available labor, or attract people from other communities. In the case of a relatively small firm, local labor will normally suffice. A good example is a building contractor who gets his workers by calling the union hiring hall. If labor is very tight, he may have to pay a premium above union wages, but if there is some unemployment, an offer of the union scale will provide him with an adequate supply of labor.

The situation is somewhat more complicated for a firm seeking to hire non-union employees. There is no unique wage scale which it can use as a guide. However, if the firm contacts employment agencies in the area or consults the want ads, it will quickly find that there are fairly well-defined conventional rates for the grade of labor in question. At any particular time the prevailing wages for, say, stenographer-typists do not vary by much. The firm may be lucky enough to hire a capable stenographer below the market rate, but if it wants to keep her, it will have to raise her to the market, since she will soon discover that she is being underpaid in comparison with her friends in other firms. Where the labor market is only partly unionized, the non-union employer can sometimes hire below the union scale, but unless he offers some compensating non-wage advantages, he will probably have to content himself with labor of a poorer quality.

If the enterprise in question, union or non-union, is a large one and requires a great many workers, or if the local labor market is in a state of full employment, additional workers must be recruited from the outside. Unless it can hire from low-wage areas, the firm may have to offer higher wages in order to compensate the new workers for the cost of moving their homes. Again, this is not always true. Some types of labor are very mobile; for example, structural-iron workers or oil-field-development workers move about the country freely and often live in trailers, and for them, the entire country is a single labor market. But in the ordinary case, a man who is employed will not move to another city unless he is offered higher wages.*

If workers are brought in from the outside at wages above those prevailing in the locality, it will not be long before there is a general upward movement in wages. A trade union is not likely to permit new men to earn more than those already employed; indeed, if initial hiring rates are below the regular rates, it may insist that the entire wage structure be moved up to preserve the contract differential. Even in the absence of a union, employees are not apt to tolerate for long a situation in which newcomers, assuming that they are not more skilled than the existing labor force, are paid more.

Let us return now to the small building firm. Suppose it is presently employing two workers, to whom it is paying the union rate of $4 an hour, and it decides to employ a third. It calls the union and the next day the new man appears, at the same $4 rate. The wage cost of this additional employee is termed the *marginal cost of labor*. In this case, the marginal cost is equal to the average wage cost of $4

---

* We are leaving out of consideration such things as climate or personal circumstances which might induce people to move for the same—or even less—money.

an hour, but this is by no means always so. If, for example, no local men were available and it was essential to bring men in from an area where the going rate was $4.50 an hour, or if a premium had to be paid to induce someone to move, the marginal cost would clearly be higher than prevailing average wages.*

In our analysis, we will concentrate on the situation in which an additional supply of employees can be obtained at locally prevailing wage rates or, in technical terms, where marginal and average labor costs are equal. This is the more common case, particularly when there is as much unemployment as we have had in the United States for the past decade. However, one must not lose sight of the fact that where labor is in short supply, the cost of hiring additional workers may impart a sharp upward trend to the prevailing wage level.

The demand for labor is derived from the demand for the product produced by that labor. Of course, labor does not receive the entire proceeds from sale of the product. There must be compensation to the other factors of production—materials, capital, management. But other things being equal, the greater the value of the goods produced and sold, the more labor can expect in wages.

Note that the compensation to labor, as well as to the other factors, depends upon the value of goods *sold*. A firm will not pay to have commodities produced, no matter how efficient the production process, if it is unable to market them.

Take a factory, or other type of enterprise of a fixed

---

* This is true not only because of the higher wage paid to the new man, but also because of the possibility that the present employees may have to be brought up to the $4.50 rate paid to the new man. If the firm can keep the wages of the new man secret, it may be able to avoid giving a raise to the older employees, but many firms do not want to risk antagonizing their employees in this way, since it is difficult to prevent wage information from spreading, and almost impossible where a union is involved.

size, that is, one in which capital equipment or floor space cannot be enlarged without a substantial delay to allow for ordering equipment and constructing additions. Beyond a certain level of employment, there will be a tendency for output per worker to fall as additional workers are put on the job. This is one of the oldest ideas in economics: the law of diminishing returns. This law refers to the common experience that overcrowding, inefficiency, and loss of productivity will result from increasing one factor of production—labor, capital, or land—without at the same time increasing either of the other factors of production. If we define the increase in output resulting from the hiring of an additional worker (all other factor inputs remaining unchanged) as the *marginal physical productivity* of that worker, we can say that there is a tendency for marginal physical productivity to decline as more and more workers are hired.

Note the condition in the above sentence: all other factor inputs remain unchanged. If, without changing the size of its labor force, a firm uses additional capital equipment, both the average productivity (total output divided by the number of workers) and the marginal productivity of labor are almost certain to rise. To a considerable extent, labor and capital are substitutable for one another in the production process. The combination of men and machines actually employed will depend on the relative cost and productivity of each. When labor is relatively cheap, a good deal of it is used. As it becomes more expensive, there is a tendency to substitute capital for it. This cannot always be done immediately, for equipment already in place may not lend itself to modification in the direction of labor saving. But at least when new plant and equipment are installed, the latest technology made economically feasible by the increased cost of labor will be introduced.

The possibility of capital-labor substitution suggests a major limitation on the power of trade unions to raise wages, one that has already been alluded to in somewhat different terms. If unions push wages up without heed to the cost impact, the demand for labor will decline as employers resort to capital substitution, and employment opportunities will be reduced. It is sometimes argued that American unions, through their aggressive wage policies, have in fact stimulated a rate of technological change in American industry beyond that which would have taken place in the absence of unionism.

At the same time, however, labor productivity rises with capital investment. This helps to explain a seeming paradox: the number of people at work has increased rapidly, yet the marginal physical productivity of labor has risen instead of fallen, as one might have expected. The reason is that the capital stock has grown more rapidly than the labor force, so that each worker is now equipped with more and better machinery than in the past. However, employment problems may arise as a result of investment in labor-saving equipment.

The marginal-productivity concept developed thus far refers to the physical output of goods. But there is another element which may also contribute to declining marginal productivity of labor. The price that a firm can get for its products depends in part upon the quantity offered for sale. If a firm is small, or if the market is very large, it will not have to worry about this, and can count on selling all it can produce at the ruling market price. But a large firm, or one that operates in a restricted market, may well find it necesssary to lower its prices in order to increase sales.* This would be the case, for example, for many companies producing various consumer durable goods—automobiles, refrigerators, and other household appliances. Therefore, when the firm expands output through expanding its plant and hiring additional labor, it may discover, when it comes to marketing the increased output, that prices must be cut,

---

* This assumes, of course, that the general price level is stable. If all prices are moving up, the firms in question would raise their prices less than they might otherwise have done.

so that the increased revenue associated with the additional workers hired will be declining as a result. This increased revenue is termed the *marginal revenue product of labor*. As in the case of marginal physical product, it will tend to fall as a firm expands its output and sales through adding workers to fixed plant and equipment. But it may also rise, despite the lower unit return from sales, if capital equipment is expanded rapidly enough, in relation to the labor force, to offset the decline in sales revenue.

If both supply and demand for labor can be determined along the lines indicated (supply in relation to wages offered, demand on the basis of the contribution of successive increments of labor to the firm's revenue) the firm is in a position to determine the level of employment which will yield the maximum profit. Let us, for example, take a retail shoe chain which is trying to decide how many employees to hire at a new shop it is opening.* It is under contract with a retail shoe clerks' union, and a survey of the local labor market reveals that it will be able to secure as many clerks as it needs by offering the union rate of $2.50 an hour. The relevant labor supply schedule is shown on p. 79. Note that the marginal labor cost is unchanged at $100 per week a man; this is the consequence of the flat union wage scale and local availability of a pool of potential employees. If labor were in short supply and had either to be hired away from competitors or imported from out of town, the hourly wage rate required might rise for successive employees, and with it, the marginal labor cost.

However, there is not yet sufficient information to permit the firm to decide how many clerks to hire. For this, the information on demand, shown on p. 80, is also

---

* I want to apologize in advance to any shoe merchant who may be reading these lines. The example is purely hypothetical, and has no relationship whatever to real costs and prices in this line of business.

LABOR SUPPLY SCHEDULE

(1)	(2)	(3)	(4)
			Marginal Weekly Payroll
	Hourly Wage	Total Weekly	Cost (marginal
Number of	Rate per	Payroll for	labor cost
Employees	Employee	a 40-Hour Week	from column 3)
1	$2.50	$100	$100
2	2.50	200	100
3	2.50	300	100
4	2.50	400	100
5	2.50	500	100
6	2.50	600	100

needed. These data illustrate some of the basic concepts explained above. Total sales do not increase in direct ratio to the increase in the labor force, because there is more idle time per employee as the number of employees increases—an illustration of the law of diminishing returns. Marginal physical productivity is shown in column 3, and marginal revenue productivity, in column 6. It will be noted that the latter declines more rapidly than the former because of the assumption, implicit in column 4, that in order to sell more than 330 pairs of shoes per week, it is necessary to reduce the price per pair. This particular illustration may strike one as an unrealistic representation of business practice, but the figures do serve to clarify the ideas involved.*

With the information at hand, our firm is now in a position to decide on the optimum number of shoe clerks to be hired. The rule is that as long as the hiring of an additional employee adds more to the firm's revenue than it costs to hire him, he will be added to the staff, since by doing so,

---

* It may be, for example, that additional sales will entail a relatively greater increase in advertising or other sales cost, thus reducing the marginal revenue product to an even greater extent. This and other possible complications are omitted in order to highlight the meaning of the marginal productivity of labor.

LABOR DEMAND SCHEDULE

(1) Number of Employees	(2) Total Pairs of Shoes Sold per Week	(3) Additional Pairs of Shoes Sold per Week (marginal physical product)	(4) Selling Price per Pair of Shoes	(5) Total Weekly Revenue	(6) Marginal Weekly Revenue (marginal revenue product)
1	120	120	$9.00	$1080	$1080
2	210	90	9.00	1890	810
3	280	70	9.00	2520	630
4	330	50	9.00	2970	450
5	360	30	8.50	3060	90
6	370	10	8.50	3145	85

profits are increased. If, on the other hand, the wage cost of the marginal worker exceeds the revenue associated with his employment, he will not be hired, since to do so would result in a reduction of profits.

Given the facts of our example, four men would constitute the optimum staff for the shop. In the case of the fifth man, the marginal cost of hiring him is $100 a week, while the marginal revenue that would result from his being hired would be only $90 a week. The disparity is even greater for the sixth man.

If a part-time person could be hired for $90 a week, and if his marginal productivity on a part-time basis was equal to that of the fifth full-time worker shown in the table above (30 pairs of shoes), it would pay the firm to do so. At that point, where the marginal cost of labor equaled the marginal revenue productivity of labor, employment would be at an equilibrium, for the firm could not hire more or fewer employees without reducing its profits. This is the only level of employment compatible with the assumption that the firm's goal is to maximize its profits.*

* Comparing total revenue and total payroll cost will not permit the firm to determine whether it is maximizing its profits, since

. . .

All of this sounds so precise and unambiguous that one may be at a loss to understand why it was necessary to issue a warning at the outset that wage and employment theory is not a completely settled branch of economics. The reason is that the results flow from certain assumptions, and if these assumptions do not correspond with reality, the results will be of little practical value. It is essential, therefore, that the nature of these assumptions be appreciated. They are:

1. Business firms are motivated primarily by the goal of maximum profits. If some other goal is a more basic motivating factor, for example, the desire for power or size, or if firms are satisfied to earn a conventional rate of profit in the interest of survival, and not necessarily maximum possible profits, the point of equality of marginal cost and marginal revenue has no significance insofar as employment is concerned. The majority of economists believe that while business motives may be mixed, the profit drive is the principal one in Western society, that it is sufficiently strong to validate the theory.

2. Business firms make marginal calculations. The numerical example given above is based upon the assumption that the shoe firm in question could and did calculate its marginal wage cost and marginal revenue product. It has been argued variously that firms think in terms of *average* rather than *marginal* cost and revenue; that they cannot possibly estimate the relevant marginal quantities (how can General Motors determine the cost of hiring one more worker, or the marginal revenue associated with his employment?); that the size of the labor force depends on the

---

labor cost is only a portion of total costs. Costs of manufacturing, transportation, advertising, store rental, etc., must be taken into account as well. If column 4 of the Labor Demand Schedule were the "net profit per unit realized before sales labor cost," the optimum employment level could be determined with reference to payroll costs alone.

technology of the machinery used, and cannot be varied without changing the machine setup (in our example, the physical size of the shop would determine the number of salesmen to be hired).

In fact, few firms make explicit marginal calculations. But the counterargument is that businessmen do think in marginal terms, or at least behave as though they thought in this manner, and that unless they did, there would be no logical limit to size or curb on expansion; that only through marginal calculations can a firm be certain that it is maximizing its profits. The theory rests upon a chain of deductive reasoning, the links of which cannot be checked experimentally. Looking from the end result, however, one can infer from success or failure whether a firm is indeed using the marginal rule—at least this is what proponents of the theory believe.

3. The labor market is similar in its essentials to the product market. This assumption permits us to construct a schedule in which the supply of labor responds to changes in the wage rate. However, critics of this point of view have pointed to the many imperfections in the labor market that make it impossible to determine the relationship of labor supply and wages with any degree of precision. In our example, we have begged the question by assuming that the firm could secure all the clerks it needed at the union rate. This would be true only under limited circumstances. Among the factors that would complicate a firm's determination of its marginal labor costs are the following:

a. We assumed that all the employees were equal in ability and skill. This may be more or less true in selling shoes (though I am certain that shoe salesmen would contradict me), but most firms employ persons of greatly varying skills and ability to perform similar work, which renders the problem of calculating marginal productivity much more difficult. Moreover, many firms customarily fill vacancies, except those at the bottom of the ladder, by promotion from within rather than by hiring in the open market. This makes the labor-supply schedule largely dependent upon the nature of the existing work force, rather than upon the labor pool in the area or elsewhere.

b. The supply schedule of labor is premised on the assumption that in accepting new employment or changing jobs, people are concerned mainly with money income, including fringe benefits (to the extent that they can be estimated in monetary terms) as well as wages. Analysis of labor mobility has led some research workers to the conclusion that money income is just one of a number of factors determining willingness to accept jobs. Such things as job security, working conditions, ease of commuting, friends and relatives in the plant, and the reputation of the firm as a good or bad employer, are some of the considerations that influence employment decisions. If this is true, the construction of a labor-supply schedule becomes much more complicated than merely estimating the response of people to various wage rates offered.

c. The labor market may be transformed by the existence of trade unions. If there is a union rate that is well-enforced, the labor-supply schedule may easily be determined for each particular skill as long as there is not an overall shortage of labor. But the union may insist that workers falling within fairly broad occupational categories be paid the same wage rate, and it may also prevent the employer from reflecting varying degrees of personal ability in differential wages. A good example of the latter is the union hiring hall often found in the maritime industry and the building trades. Here, the employer will have greater difficulty in estimating potential marginal productivity; a good man will produce more than a poor one and may be worth hiring if a close calculation is involved, but the employer cannot know in advance.*

There are answers to all of these points, but they would

* Some employers attempt to get around this by asking for employees by name. This is possible in many construction trades, but the maritime unions usually do not permit it.

take us too far afield. The arguments can be summed up by saying that while all the complications cited are real ones, when all is said and done, men and women are greatly influenced by earnings prospects in choosing employment, and the size of the paycheck is a major factor in inducing them to move. Labor markets are not at all uniform with respect to the ease or difficulty of predicting the response of labor supply to wage changes, but all things considered, they seem to be sufficiently subject to economic forces to make the concept of a labor-supply schedule meaningful. A construction contracting firm can make bids for jobs in many parts of the country on the basis of fairly accurate labor-cost estimates. A manufacturing firm, by taking into account its past experience and current economic conditions, will normally have a fairly shrewd idea of the costs involved in hiring more labor. On balance, the assumptions of the theory do not appear to be so contradictory to the facts of life as to make us reject it. At the same time, it is well to remember that it is quite general, and that in any given situation the immediate circumstances may contain elements which result in invalid predictions when the theory is applied to that particular case.

A further major limitation of the theory should be noted. The labor supply and demand schedules relate to a particular period of time, usually a short one, and are based upon stable price and wage levels. If there is a change in either prices or wages, the entire situation may be altered. Suppose that in our example the price of shoes rose by $1.00 a pair in each case of the Labor Demand Schedule, column 4, with no change in wage rates. The marginal weekly revenue associated with the fifth employee would become $120, exceeding the marginal cost of $100, and making it profitable to hire five men. On the other hand, if the general level of wages or the added wage cost of securing additional workers went up, profit maximization might dictate the hiring of fewer than four employees.

While prices are more likely to fluctuate in the short run than wages, both will change in time, and usually in the same direction. The net effect on the equilibrium employment level depends on which moves more. If prices are rising more rapidly than wages, marginal revenue product will rise more rapidly than marginal labor cost, and it will pay to hire more workers, and vice versa. But each time wages or prices change, new schedules of labor supply and demand must be drawn up to reflect the new levels.

Suppose that wages and prices do not change, but that for some reason which does not entail additional capital investment—better arrangement of the stock, increasing experience, greater effort—sales of shoes per employee increase. (This would be reflected in the table on p. 80 in increases in columns 2, 5, and 6.) It might well be that it would then become profitable to employ five or even more persons, depending upon the exact calculation. An increase in labor productivity may thus offset rising wages, and act in the same direction as rising prices, in terms of affording greater employment opportunities.

Finally, it is necessary to consider the complications that enter into wage-employment determination when we relax the assumption that the firm holds its capital stock constant. A decision to expand plant and equipment, or to install more advanced equipment, may have the following consequences, among others:

1. In all likelihood, the new capital will increase the average productivity of the labor force, if no additional employees are added. In our shoe-chain outlet, more floor space and automatic stock-handling equipment would undoubtedly raise the weekly sales of each employee, assuming that there are sufficient customers.

2. Marginal physical productivity would probably rise as well for all the employees in the shoe example. But this is not necessarily true of all capital expansion. For example, if highly automated machinery is installed in place of a

process formerly requiring a good deal of labor, diminishing returns may set in very rapidly after a small crew has been hired.

3. Even if marginal physical productivity for all present employees is raised by additional investment, it does not follow that more employees will be hired at unchanged wage levels. We have already noted that other costs in addition to labor enter into a firm's revenue calculations. Rent and interest on capital are costs, and they go up with expansion of facilities, thus reducing the profit margin on each unit of sales. Thus, higher sales per employee may be more than offset by the smaller revenue associated with each employee, calling for a reduction rather than an increase in staff.

Once we have all the facts about the nature of the plant and equipment to be used, marginal-productivity theory permits us to reach certain conclusions about employment and wages, within the limitations set forth. New investment and alterations to existing equipment are not undertaken every day, so that the theory has considerable relevance. But once the decision to review the labor-capital mix is made, a Pandora's box is opened. Conflicting employment effects are set in motion, and the ultimate outcome will depend on which of them is strongest.

It may be useful at this point to attempt to use the theory for analyzing the impact of minimum-wage legislation on employment. The Fair Labor Standards Act, which was enacted in 1938, started with a wage of 25 cents an hour as a required minimum for firms engaged in interstate commerce. Subsequent congressional action has raised the minimum to the current level of $1.25 an hour, a figure that the AFL–CIO is seeking to increase still further. Let us leave aside the moral arguments in favor of a higher minimum wage ($1.25 an hour yields a poverty-level income on a full-year basis*) and concentrate on the economic implications of a change to, let us say, $1.50.

All firms which now pay below $1.50 an hour, and there are many of them in certain low-wage manufacturing industries and in service trades, would be affected immediately. The theory tells us that a certain number of workers would have to be laid off until marginal revenue product equaled $1.50 an hour for each firm (equivalent to moving up column 6 of the Labor Demand Schedule table). The net result of the new law would thus be to reduce employment opportunities.

Analysis of past changes in the minimum wage reveals that some loss of employment has indeed taken place in consequence of wage increases, at least temporarily. However, it has not been possible, even after several exhaustive investigations undertaken by the U.S. Department of Labor, to determine the effects on employment with any degree of precision. Among the adjustments that may have enabled low-wage employers to retain their previous staff, or to discharge fewer workers than might have been anticipated, are the following:

1. The wage increase may have been absorbed out of profits. This would be particularly true in situations where wages being paid were actually below marginal productivity because of lack of bargaining power on the part of the workers, as, for example, in a small town with a single major employer.

2. Output per worker may have been raised by improvements in management, greater effort on the part of labor, or the substitution of capital for labor. Any measures that cut costs would tend to raise the marginal revenue product of labor.

3. Prices may have been increased, offsetting the higher

---

* This wage, per hour, would yield $2600 a year, which is below the generally accepted poverty level of $3000 a year or less. See p. 123.

wage minimum. The period since the enactment of the Fair Labor Standards Act has been characterized by a rising price level, and although this has not been true of every year, or of every industry, the general trend has been sufficient to take much of the sting out of the successive increases in the legal minimum.

This example illustrates both the value and limitations of wage theory. In the short run, when the economic environment is stable, the theory enables us to make some useful predictions about the interaction of wages and employment at the level of the individual firm. But it is dangerous to apply the theory mechanistically, and particularly to draw policy conclusions from it, when such basic economic factors as prices and the ratio of capital to labor are subject to change. This is why it is still possible, after almost thirty years of study, for economists to continue to argue about what seems to be so simple a matter as the impact of minimum-wage legislation on employment.

V

Wages, Employment,

and Inflation

In the preceding chapters, we have been concerned primarily with the determination of the optimum employment level by the individual firm. The next question to be faced is this: Can we move from the single firm to the economy as a whole simply by adding the individual labor demand-and-supply schedules? As we have seen, under certain circumstances a single firm may be able to hire more labor if it can pay lower wages. Does it follow from this that the remedy for unemployment is a general reduction in the wage level?

There are economists and businessmen who think that this is indeed the case. They find in the downward inflexibility of wages caused by worker resistance to wage cuts and in minimum-wage laws the major reason for our failure to achieve full employment. But this view is rejected by the majority.

If one accepts the assumptions of marginal-productivity wage theory, as exemplified in the tables on pages 79 and 80, it is clear that a firm will tend to hire additional men if it succeeds in getting workers to accept lower wage rates.

However, if all the firms in the economy, or a substantial number of them, were to reduce wages simultaneously, the amount of purchasing power available would tend to fall by a corresponding amount, since wages are for the most part normally spent soon after they are earned. The reduction in purchasing power may be partly offset by the earnings of the new employees, though the extent to which that turns out to be true depends upon their previous status. If they were not working at all, the effect will be greatest, but if they were getting unemployment compensation or some other form of unemployment assistance, or were working part-time, the offset addition to purchasing power would be less.

There is a distinct possibility, however, that there will not be sufficient new purchasing power to match the added output resulting from the employment of more workers; in fact, there may even be a net decline in purchasing power, depending upon the amount of the wage reduction. The result would be a general decline in the demand for labor, rather than an increase. Something of the sort seems to have happened during the Great Depression that began in 1929. Wages were pretty well maintained until 1931, but the large wage cuts introduced in that year not only did not improve the employment situation, but resulted in a deepening of the crisis.

If a general reduction in wages is not the answer from a theoretical point of view (to say nothing of the tremendous practical difficulties of effectuating such a policy), what about adopting the reverse policy of *raising* wages as a means of increasing purchasing power? This idea is often advanced by trade-union officials as the simplest means of stimulating employment. Unfortunately, wages are costs as well as purchasing power. The individual firm will find that its labor costs have risen by the full amount of the wage increases, but part of the increased wages may be saved by the recipients, so that purchasing power may not rise sufficiently to offset the increased cost. The net result may be no additional employment, or even a reduction in employment, depending again upon the relative movement of wages and prices.

It would appear, therefore, that labor demand-and-supply schedules for the entire economy are much more difficult to construct, both conceptually and practically, than for the individual firm. Moreover, they are not independent of one another, as we assumed they were for the firm, because of the dual role of wages as costs and purchasing power. At the level of the national economy it is also necessary to take into account the role of the government, which through a variety of mechanisms, including the budget, credit and monetary policy, and direct welfare payments to individual citizens, can greatly influence economic trends, including employment.

A full discussion of wage-price-employment relationships in the national economy would take us far beyond the confines of this single volume.* We will confine ourselves in this chapter to a consideration of the wage-price inflation issue, and to the impact of trade unions on both wages and prices; in the following chapter we will take up the relationship between aggregate demand, or purchasing power, and employment.

Compensation to wage and salary earners constitutes about 70 percent of our national income. Labor is usually the major cost element to a producer or merchandiser, though the exact proportion of labor to total costs varies among industries. An increase in wages and salaries is bound to increase costs, and thus to put pressure on prices. However, wages and prices do not move together with any degree of exactitude. If they did so, real income would always remain the same, and we have already seen that on

---

* For some aspects of this problem, the reader is referred to two previous books in this series: Robert L. Heilbroner and Peter L. Bernstein, *A Primer on Government Spending,* and Peter L. Bernstein, *A Primer on Money, Banking and Gold.*

the contrary, real incomes have risen persistently in the United States.

The gear mechanism that enables wages and prices to move at different rates is to be found in productivity. An increase in output per worker can offset increased wages and leave labor costs unchanged. From 1960 to 1964, average labor productivity* in the United States rose by 3.5 percent per annum. During the same period, compensation per man-hour worked increased by almost the same amount: 3.3 percent in manufacturing, 3.6 percent in the private economy as a whole. Labor costs were thus quite stable, and this enabled business firms to keep prices from rising. It is true that the consumer price index went up by 1.2 percent a year on the average, but when quality improvements and the introduction of new products are taken into account, this figure does not represent a significant increase in living costs. A nice balance between wages and prices was thus achieved, and the money-wage increases were translated directly into real-wage increases.

The general formula for price stability was spelled out in 1962 by the Council of Economic Advisers in the form of wage-price guideposts for labor and management to follow:

1. The general guide for wages is that the percentage increase in total employee compensation per man-hour be equal to the national trend rate of increase in output per man-hour. If each industry follows this guidepost, unit labor costs in the overall economy will maintain a constant average.

2. The general guide for prices calls for stable prices in industries enjoying the same productivity growth as the average for the economy; rising prices in industries with smaller than average productivity gains; and

---

* Productivity can be measured in a number of different ways. The most useful one for our purposes is in terms of value of output per man-hour, corrected for changes in the price level.

declining prices in industries with greater than average
productivity gains.*

The Council pointed out that exceptions to the wage
guides may be necessary to permit an industry to expand
its labor force or to increase substandard wages, while on
the price side, increases above the guideposts might be
needed to offset rising non-labor costs or to attract new
capital to the industry.

These guideposts, although promulgated by a government agency, are in no sense mandatory. Many collective
agreements have exceeded the wage guidepost limitations,
and most firms do not feel obligated to follow the indicated
price limitations. Yet it is remarkable that on the average
for the past few years the sum of all private and public
actions have pretty well conformed to the guidepost relationships. This is in sharp distinction to the 1950's when
wages outran productivity, to say nothing of the years
1945 to 1950.

Prior to the present era of price stability, there was a
great debate on the causes of inflation. Some blamed it on
the trade-union appetite for higher money wages, pushing
costs and prices up. Others pointed instead to excessive
demand generated by too great an availability of purchasing power in the face of inadequate production. This issue
of "cost push" versus "demand pull" has abated temporarily, at least until the next bout of inflation, but it was never
settled satisfactorily. In many countries other than the
United States it continues to be a serious problem.

The rapid price increases from 1945 to 1948 were
clearly due to excess demand. A great deal of purchasing
power had been built up during the war when people were
earning good money with little to spend it on. When consumer-goods production, particularly of automobiles, was
resumed, there was a mad scramble to purchase. There

* *Annual Report of the Council of Economic Advisers*, 1965, p.
108.

was another large price advance during the Korean War, mainly the result of anticipatory buying by consumers who remembered the shortages of the earlier war years and wanted to stock up. Since 1953, however, there has been no real shortage of goods, yet on several occasions, notably in 1956 and 1957, prices resumed an upward course.*

It is difficult to escape the conclusion that since 1953, cost push has been the principal cause of price inflation, and that collectively bargained wage increases have been a major element behind the wage-cost rise. The Council of Economic Advisers noted in its 1965 Annual Report:

> Many unions have become powerful, and they are in a position to hold their own in the periodic collective bargaining process. Although they are constrained by market forces, powerful unions can, and sometimes do, obtain wage increases that outrun productivity even when labor supply is relatively abundant.

The steel industry is often cited as one in which a powerful union has been able to gain large wage increases despite the existence of unemployment. A group of distinguished economists, after analyzing the experience of Western Europe and the United States, reached the following conclusions:

> . . . we believe that wages have generally risen faster than they would have done solely under the influence of demand in a competitive market . . . we have not found evidence of any unique and predictable relationship be-

* Consumer prices in the United States rose by 6.3 percent from 1956 to 1958, and by 16 percent for the entire period 1953–1964. By comparison with other nations, however, this rise was moderate. For a shorter period, 1953–1961, there was a price increase of 38 percent in France, 28 percent in Sweden, and 25 percent in Great Britain. In some countries of Latin America, price inflation was truly astronomical during these years: 507 percent in Brazil, 1153 percent in Chile, 570 percent in Argentina, and 3500 percent in Bolivia!

tween demand and the rate of increase in wages. In our view, the pressure exerted in wage negotiations and the use made of the wage negotiating machinery has been a vital factor in the equation.*

Inflation is often regarded as an evil to be avoided at all costs, though in the next chapter it will be argued that a slowly rising price level may be preferable to unemployment, if a choice must be made. Let us assume, however, that price stability is a paramount objective, and inquire into the significance of this goal for wage-setting mechanisms.

Despite what has been quoted above from the Council of Economic Advisers and the OECD group, some doubts have been expressed about the ability of unions to influence wages to any significant extent. The question may be looked at from three different points of view: labor's share in the national income, the relative income of union and non-union workers, and the general level of wages.

From 1929 to 1964, labor's share in the national income increased from 58 to 71 percent. During the same period, trade-union membership rose from 3.4 million to more than 17 million, so that one might be tempted to infer a direct cause-and-effect relationship between the two. However, the increased share of compensation is probably due in large part to other factors. One of the principal causes is a decline in self-employment and a corresponding increase in the proportion of the labor force working for salaries and wages. Perhaps the most striking manifestation of this trend is the decline of the agricultural labor force, which in 1929 was predominantly self-employed, from 21.5 percent of the total labor force in

* Organization for European Economic Co-operation, *The Problem of Rising Prices*, 1961, p. 50. This organization has since been renamed the Organization for Economic Cooperation and Development (OECD). It might be noted that some economists maintain that demand pull, rather than cost push, has been responsible for the post-1953 inflation, but this is a minority view.

that year to 6.7 percent in 1964. However, this is true out-side agriculture as well: for example, since 1947, the num-ber of self-employed workers has risen insignificantly, whereas the non-agricultural labor force increased by al-most 16 million persons.

The share of profits, from which much of the increase in wages might have been expected to come if union activity were the main lever of change, remained almost un-changed over the period. The shares of interest and rent declined substantially, indicating an income shift away from propertied groups, but this has probably been due chiefly to price inflation, which bears most heavily on the owners of fixed obligations.

But national-income statistics tell only part of the story. The trade-union movement has been the spearhead in the drive for shorter hours, fringe benefits, and greater security of employment. The standard 40-hour week for manual labor first came in during the 1930's, and a further reduc-tion is now in the offing. Paid vacations for blue-collar workers were rare prior to 1940, but now they are almost universal. On these two counts there has been a relative shift of leisure time to workers.

Fringe benefits are included in the national-income cate-gory of compensation of employees, and their expansion may have something to do with the increased share of this type of income. Apart from the totals, however, there has been substantial change in the distribution of these bene-fits. Corporate pensions to executives are of long standing, but it required extensive strike action to induce the larger companies to extend the privilege to their blue-collar workers. Medical benefits, supplements to unemployment compensation, and other non-wage benefits for manual workers were similarly the result of union pressure. These might have come even in the absence of unionism, but it may be noted that when unions were weak or non-existent, the rate at which they were being introduced was remark-ably slow. However one interprets the national-income data, there is some warrant for the belief, on the basis of these benefits, that unionism has been an effective force in improving the economic status of the manual worker.

As for the relative income of union members, there is the possibility that even though unions raise the wages of their members, they do so at the expense of non-union workers. If there were no unions, would wages in the presently unionized plants and industries be relatively lower than they are compared with non-union plants and industries? Some of those who have studied the problem believe that when unions are first organized, they manage to secure a wage advantage for their members, but that thereafter, the union premium remains stable. Others deny that unions are able to maintain any wage advantage in the long run, arguing that observable differences are due to higher productivity and a greater degree of monopoly in the unionized sectors. One of the facts that makes it difficult to obtain a precise answer is that unions have considerable influence on non-union wage levels. Unless there is very substantial unemployment, non-union firms will have to match union wage advances in order to keep their workers. Some firms have even paid above union levels to prevent their employees from unionizing.

The upshot of the paragraphs immediately above is that trade unions have some influence over the distribution of income among different groups in the community and between union and non-union workers, though the extent of the influence cannot be determined statistically. The facts are much less ambiguous with respect to the general level of wages. Trade unions, through their bargaining power, push wages up and contribute to the cost-push effect on prices. A price stabilization policy which is to have any chance of success must take collective bargaining into account.

The wage-price guideposts which were outlined above represent the present stabilization policy of the United States government. At about the time this policy was developed, the OECD economic experts referred to earlier advocated very much the same program for other nations as well:

> . . . the authorities themselves must have a reasonably precise view, estimated by the best means which they can devise, of the average increase in wages that is appropriate to the economic situation and consistent with stability of the price level. This view will necessarily depend primarily on experience and expectations regarding the longer-run rate of productivity increase in the economy. . . . Having such a view, getting it known by the interested parties and mobilizing support for it as an objective towards which to work, is the essence of having a wage policy.*

It is worth repeating that this policy does not imply direct governmental control over wages and prices, as we had during wartime. Rather, its rationale is the public announcement of wage-price norms to which key labor and management groups are expected to pay attention when they are engaged in collective bargaining. Failure to do this does not entail legal penalties, but public opinion may be mobilized by government economic officials, or in particularly important cases—steel and autos, for example—by the President of the United States, against excessive wage or price increases. Labor or management may decide in the end that the particular economic situation requires the guidelines to be breached, but neither one will make this decision without preparing ample justification for its action. This is in sharp contrast to the way similar decisions were made less than a decade ago. The prevailing attitude then was that wage and price policy were purely private matters; it is now conceded that a direct public interest is involved.

It is much too soon to say that the guideline policy has solved the problem of inflation. The period it spans is a

* OEEC, *The Problem of Rising Prices*, pp. 57–58.

short one, and other aspects of the economy were in fairly good balance. Future surges of demand, the international situation, or a reduction in unemployment, may render the economy more vulnerable to cost push.

Fortunately, our collective-bargaining system contains certain restraining elements which are likely to keep the problem within reasonable bounds. We have already referred to the ability of union leaders to appraise the market situation realistically and tailor their demands accordingly. Occasionally, wage demands which, if satisfied, may push prices up, are necessary for internal political reasons. But there is no indication that unions are irresponsible and bound to cause inflation.

The acceptance of certain criteria as the basis for wage negotiation also helps to maintain collective-bargaining stability. The profit position of a firm or industry is always an important element. Unions recognize that profits are essential to the health of industry, though excessive profits may be tempting targets leading to excessive wage demands. The tying of wages to productivity, the so-called annual improvement factor, explicitly recognizes the role of productivity in the wage-price relationship and has helped focus attention on this critical magnitude.

Changes in the cost of living inevitably affect the course of wage negotiation, and this is as true of individual as of collective bargaining. Rapid upward movements are likely to engender demands for wage compensation in order to maintain real wages intact. In actual fact, wages tend to lag behind living costs in periods of rapid inflation, and contracts which provide for periodic wage adjustment on the basis of cost-of-living index movements merely shorten the lag.

It is sometimes asserted that collective agreements keep wages below what the market would call for when there is an upward price tendency, since they determine wages for a fixed term of one or two years. In a tight labor market, however, wages tend to move up beyond contract rates, giving rise to a phenomenon known as "wage drift." This comes about through an upward creep in piece-rate earnings and in wage premiums paid to keep workers from leaving and to attract new ones. Wage drift has not been a serious matter in the United States since the war, because our labor market has not been tight, but in a country like Sweden, where unemployment has all but vanished, it has been of constant concern to government, employers, and trade unions alike.

Finally, employers should not be pictured as defenseless, passive parties in the bargaining process. They are well aware of their interests, and if demands are made with which they cannot live, they have the alternative of taking a strike.

There are other limits to cost-push inflation beyond collective bargaining. The government can call a halt to price increases by a variety of means at its disposal, though these may not always be feasible politically. The international trade position may also curb expansion; if prices rise too rapidly, the ability to export is reduced, the balance of payments may become unfavorable, and imports are curbed. We have emphasized the wage-price aspects of the inflationary problem, but it is not correct to look upon them as the only contributing factor.

In Part II we have examined employment and wage determination for the individual firm, and arrived at a useful theoretical formulation of the relationship between them. This wage theory of the firm, however, cannot be applied directly to the national economy; there are many complexities which would make this a dubious procedure. A simple general theory that works on the level of the national economy is a much more difficult matter.

By a process of experimentation, the United States seems to have arrived at a combination of collective bargaining and non-compulsory government action which has given the country an enviable record of economic stability for a decade. The system gives ample scope to free market forces, and at the same time provides for recognition of the public interest. We must reserve judgment on whether it will continue to work as well in the future. Its main blemish, and it is a large one, is the inability to eliminate unemployment and poverty, and it is to these subjects that we now turn.

Part

III

UNEMPLOYMENT
AND POVERTY

VI

Who Are the Unemployed?

The two decades since 1945 are the most satisfactory in the history of the United States, from an economic point of view. There has been sustained growth, and the 5 percent average annual increase in gross national product since 1961 is little short of spectacular, given our level of development. Over the twenty postwar years, the output of goods and services for each person in the country has risen by 35 percent.

Despite the affluence that is visible all around us, the twin problems of unemployment and poverty remain unsolved. Unemployment averaged 5.2 percent of the labor force during 1964, which meant that at any given time during the year, about 4 million people were unable to find work.* The Council of Economic Advisers has estimated that 35 million Americans, one-fifth of the entire population, are still living under conditions of poverty. This dis-

-----

* This is not to say that only 4 million *individuals* experienced some unemployment during the year. There were probably from 12 to 16 million who were out of work at some time or other in 1964.

crepancy in opportunity and income, wider than that which prevails in many other industrial countries, is beginning to arouse the nation's conscience. As a result, there is some hope that we may at last eradicate the social evils of unemployment and poverty and render obsolete the belief that the poor must always be with us.

Unemployment appears to be a simple phenomenon at first glance. But when one attempts to measure it, a host of questions arise. Is everyone not working, but capable of working, unemployed regardless of his desire to work or not to work? Are part-time workers unemployed? How should individuals who can get jobs but are holding out for better ones be treated? What about persons who are working far below their skills and capabilities? These are but a few of the questions that must be answered before enumeration begins.

There were no national unemployment statistics prior to 1940. Estimates based on local surveys indicate that unemployment may have been as high as 25 percent of the labor force in 1933, at the depth of the depression. Since 1940, the Census Bureau has been making monthly sample surveys of the labor force, so that our data are now much more accurate. All persons 14 years of age and over who are in the labor force are classified as either employed or unemployed, the latter on the basis of the following definition:

Unemployed persons include those who did not work at all during the survey week and were looking for work. Those who had made efforts to find jobs within the preceding 60-day period—such as by registering at a public or private employment agency, writing letters of application, canvassing for work, etc.—and who, during the survey week, were awaiting the results of those efforts are also regarded as looking for work. Also included as un-

employed are those who did not work at all during the
survey week and—

    a. Were waiting to be called back to a job from which
       they had been laid off; or

    b. Were waiting to report to a new wage or salary job
       scheduled to start within the following 30 days (and
       were not in school during the survey week); or

    c. Would have been looking for work except that they
       were temporarily ill or believed no work was avail-
       able in their line of work or in the community.

This definition of unemployment contains many arbi-
trary elements. A man who worked even one hour during
the survey week would not be counted as unemployed.
Persons not working because of bad weather are considered employed, while those on short layoffs are unemployed. Nevertheless, the definition has withstood the test
of time, in that most economists do, in fact, regard it as a
satisfactory way of drawing the line.

In statistical terms, unemployment is usually presented
as a percentage of the labor force. The annual averages
from 1945 to 1964 are shown in the table on p. 108. Up to
1954, unemployment was relatively low, apart from a
bulge in 1949–1950. But since 1954, the annual rate has
never been below 4 percent, and for most of the decade it
has exceeded 5 percent. Some unemployment is unavoidable in a dynamic economy, but there is general agreement
that the rates since 1954 are too high.

Unemployment is not spread equally among all groups
in the labor force. The following are particularly prone to
its risks:

Younger workers. The unemployment rate for teenagers
(16–19) has been running at about three times the average
for all workers, while unemployment among workers in
their early twenties (20–24) has exceeded the average by
50 percent or more. There are a number of reasons for

UNEMPLOYMENT AS A PERCENTAGE OF THE
CIVILIAN LABOR FORCE, 1945–1964
(ANNUAL AVERAGES)

Year	Percent	Year	Percent
1945	1.9[a]	1955	4.4
1946	3.9[a]	1956	4.2
1947	3.6[a]	1957	4.3
1948	3.8	1958	6.8
1949	5.9	1959	5.5
1950	5.3	1960	5.6
1951	3.3	1961	6.7
1952	3.1	1962	5.6
1953	2.9	1963	5.7
1954	5.6	1964	5.2

[a] These figures differ slightly in concept from the later ones.
SOURCES: *Historical Statistics of the United States; 1965 Annual Report of the Council of Economic Advisers.*

this: difficulties of adjustment in the transition from school to work, lack of the skills increasingly being required of new entrants into the labor force, vulnerability to layoff under union contracts because of the operation of seniority clauses. Large numbers of young workers, representing the postwar baby boom, are entering the labor market—500,-000 in the age groups 18 and 19 years alone during 1964.* It is expected that by 1970 there will be 6 million more workers between the ages of 14 and 24 than there were in 1960.

A government report had this to say about unemployment among our youth:

Never before in our recent history has so large a proportion of teenagers started their work lives with the disadvantages of unemployment—in many cases frequent or prolonged periods of joblessness. For these, the already difficult problems of beginning a successful work career

* This increase is larger than the entire growth of this age group in the labor force between 1950 and 1963.

are increased many-fold. The experience, learning, and seniority that generally go only with stable employment are postponed, frequently into the adult years, when the responsibilities of marriage and a family add to the burdens of unemployment.*

While putting younger people to work does offer special problems, particularly with their present great influx into the labor market, it is by no means inevitable that they should be so much more subject to unemployment than adults. In Great Britain and Sweden, unemployment among the youth is not significantly above the adult average.

Older workers. Men who lose their jobs after they have reached the age of 55 years find it more difficult to obtain re-employment than do younger men, which is reflected in a higher rate of unemployment for them.† In fact, difficulties begin at an even earlier age. This is true despite the fact that older workers enjoy the protection of union seniority agreements. Nevertheless, once they are laid off, their spells of unemployment are longer than those of younger men.

Negro workers. The rate of unemployment among Negroes substantially exceeds that of white workers. The average for whites in 1964 was 4.6 percent, and for Negroes, 9.8 percent. The disparity persists for subgroups. For example, 23 percent of Negro teenage boys (18 and 19 years) were unemployed in 1964, compared with 13.4 percent for white boys in the same age group. This difference did not exist until the mid-1950's, but is something that has developed during the past ten years.

The white-Negro unemployment differential runs through all occupational groups, and indeed, it is relatively greater

* *Manpower Report of the President,* 1965, p. 29.
† This does not seem to be true for older women. However, it may be that older women who have difficulty finding new jobs leave the labor force, which would understate the degree of unemployment among them.

among skilled than unskilled workers. While the higher overall Negro unemployment rate is partly due to the concentration of Negroes in unstable, low-skill employment, this is by no means the entire story.

Unskilled workers. There is a clear relationship between skill and education, on the one hand, and employment stability on the other. The 1964 unemployment rate was 10.6 percent for laborers, 6.5 percent for semi-skilled factory workers, 4.2 percent for craftsmen, and 1.7 percent for professional and technical workers. More education and less unemployment go together. High-school dropouts do less well in terms of stable jobs than those who go on to graduate.

While education is clearly desirable not only in terms of job opportunities, but also for its own sake, more education alone will not solve the unemployment problem. If everyone had a college education and wanted a job commensurate with his training, there would be a surplus of intellectuals and a shortage of blue-collar workers. Education pays off at present because changing technology and increased demands for professional services have combined to create a strong demand for higher skills. But in many underdeveloped countries which lack advanced industries, there is a high rate of unemployment among college graduates even though there are very few of them.

High unemployment industries. Certain industries give rise to more than their share of unemployment, either because there is a long-run decline in their demand for labor or because of seasonality or some other irregularity in their operations. Coal mining is a good example of long-run decline: employment of bituminous coal miners fell from 440,000 in 1940 to about 150,000 at present. Despite this very sharp drop in employment, the current output of coal is not far from what it was in 1940.

The coal industry is often cited as a classic case of the impact of high wages on employment. John L. Lewis, for many years the head of the United Mine Workers of America, pushed for higher wages without regard for the effect on employment. It was his belief that the fewer people who had to do the dirty and dangerous job of underground mining, the better. As a result of this policy, the once underprivileged coal miners now enjoy among the highest hourly wage rates of any large occupational group, while the mine operators, faced by rising labor costs, mechanized work that had been performed by hand for generations. The only unfortunate aspect of this sequence of events is that there are thousands of former coal miners who have not been able to find other jobs, either because they were too old or lacked the means or knowledge to move out of the coal valleys.

The construction industry, with a high degree of seasonality and irregularity of employment, poses quite a different problem. The unemployment rate for construction workers was about twice that in manufacturing in 1964. But unlike coal mining, the construction industry has been booming, and employment has risen steadily. Here, the unemployment is due to bad weather and the constant turnover of workers from one job to another.

Local areas of high unemployment. The Department of Labor regularly follows employment trends in 150 major labor market areas in the country. Several areas are far above the national unemployment average, among them the old textile cities of Massachusetts and the Appalachian region. These are areas that have long been plagued with excess unemployment, which is generally due to declining industries or exhaustion of natural resources.

Some labor market areas which were very badly hit during the 1950's have made remarkable recoveries. Detroit, for example, moved down from 15 percent unemployment in 1958 to a below-average 4.2 percent in 1964, due largely to the recovery of the auto industry. But not all were as lucky, and there are stagnant pockets of unemployment which will probably require special treatment. If these areas are not going to attract new industry, the people must move out, but it should not be forgotten that movement often entails considerable financial, social, and human cost. Homes must be sold in depressed real-estate markets and repurchased where quarters are scarce. Families may be separated while the breadwinner establishes himself in a new locale. Relatives, friends, churches, social clubs, have to be left behind. All of this may be necessary if permanent unemployment is to be avoided, but it is well to remember that labor mobility is not a painless, automatic process.

VII

Analytical Aspects of

Unemployment

The persistence of unemployment in the face of high levels of business activity has given rise to the hypothesis that the roots of the problem lie in the structure of the labor force and the economy rather than in the lack of adequate demand for goods and services. There is no doubt, as we have already seen, that unemployment falls with particular severity on certain groups, industries, and areas. It has therefore been urged that measures aimed specifically at the alleviation of unemployment among these groups is the proper approach. Those who advocate this policy argue that merely increasing aggregate demand would not work, because long before the youth, the Negroes, and the displaced coal miners found jobs, there would be serious shortages of skilled workers and professionals, among whom there was little unemployment to begin with. These shortages would create bottlenecks to expanding employment, and would also tend to push wages and prices up.

An opposite point of view, identified particularly with the Council of Economic Advisers, holds that the key to reduction of unemployment lies in the creation of sufficient overall demand in the economy to provide jobs even for marginal workers. When work is scarce and applicants are many, employers give preference to white adults, but when the pool of unemployed from whom they can hire shrinks, they have to take anyone they can get. When the average unemployment rate increases by 1 percent, the rate for Negroes and teenagers rises by about 2 percent, while the reverse is true when average unemployment is falling. For example, average unemployment for all groups rose by 2.5 percent from 1957 to 1958, whereas teenage and Negro unemployment rose by 3.6 and 4.6 percent respectively. On the other hand, during 1964, the average rate of unemployment declined by 0.5 percent, that of teenagers by 0.9 percent, and that of Negroes by 1.1 percent.

A careful study of this problem by Professor R. A. Gordon of the University of California led to the conclusion that "the period of high total unemployment in the last half-dozen years has not been characterized by an increasing concentration of unemployment among the groups that are structurally most disadvantaged in seeking jobs." * One answer to the skill-bottleneck argument is that the United States operated at a fairly low level of unemployment in the mid-1950's without running out of skilled personnel, and that employers show great ingenuity in making do with the workers they already have when forced to.

One way to test the rival theories would be to see what was happening to job vacancies when unemployment rose or fell. If an increasing average rate of unemployment were accompanied by a rise in unfilled vacancies, putting aggregate demand up would not help matters, since clearly the qualifications of the unemployed were not matching the skill specifications of the vacancies. Unfortunately, adequate job-vacancy statistics do not exist, since public employment offices handle only a small proportion of all placements.

These two views of the causes of unemployment—struc-

* *Industrial Relations,* May 1964.

tural and aggregate demand—are often stated as mutually exclusive propositions. In fact, a logical approach would lie somewhere in between. If demand were driven up to a sufficiently high level, the lame, the halt, and the blind would find employers camping on their doorsteps, entreating them to accept jobs. But high demand means great pressure on wage and price levels, and it might produce an unacceptable degree of inflation. On the other hand, little would be accomplished by training the unskilled and the displaced, and by breaking down racial barriers, if the doors to employment were barred by lack of employer interest in expanding their staffs. Structural elements and lack of sufficient demand jointly contribute to our excessively high rate of unemployment, and any successful policy must tackle the two simultaneously.

Automation has become a household word in the United States. The term is often used loosely as a synonym for technological advance, but what is new is the development of automatic control systems and electronic computers, sometimes operating in tandem. Many predictions have been made about the impact of automation on employment, ranging from a mild tendency toward displacement of labor to the virtual elimination of all human beings from the production process. George Meany, president of the AFL–CIO, warned his constituents: "Automation can be a blessing or it can be a curse. . . . There is no longer any question in my mind as to the direction in which automation is going today. There is no element of blessing in it. It is rapidly becoming a real curse to this society." Walter Reuther, head of the United Automobile Workers, expressed the fear that automation might displace 3½ million employees a year unless the economy expanded sufficiently to offset it.

Automation is essentially a continuation of the improvement in technology that has characterized Western society since the beginning of the Industrial Revolution in

Great Britain. History is filled with examples of human skills made obsolete by machines. One of the novel aspects of contemporary automation, however, is that it affects white-collar as well as manual jobs. The preparation of payrolls, check sorting and posting in banks, airline reservations, the preparation of children's report cards in schools, are a few examples of what the machine has begun to take over during the past ten years. Even more, computerized medical diagnosis may well revolutionize the discovery and treatment of disease; lawyers can already save long hours of searching for case precedents in preparing their briefs by reference to computers; a great deal of teaching is done by television; and considerable progress is being made in automatic translation from one language to another. All of these things reduce the demand for labor, but it is repetitive labor. Clerical and professional productivity is being greatly increased, and creative work should be able to take the place of routine drudgery. Despite Mr. Meany, it is difficult to see these developments as a curse.

The real question is not whether automation, and continued technological change in general, are going to transform the labor market into a vast desert, punctuated only by the whirring of automatic machinery—this will not happen—or whether the trend is good or bad, for, good or bad, its progress is inevitable. What we must know is more precise: What exactly will automation mean for the level and structure of employment? In spite of the alarms of the last few years, there are very few hard facts.

Consider, for example, the changes in skill requirements that will result from technological change, including automation. It is usually assumed that the demand for unskilled and semi-skilled work will decline, whereas higher skills will be in great demand. However, Professor James Bright of Harvard University concluded, after a careful study of the impact of automation on thirteen sample plants, that no substantial increase in the average level of skill required had resulted. A machine monitor is not necessarily more skilled than a machine operative. Computer programing and operating do not require long training or educational background. Some aspects of managerial and professional work are even being downgraded by the management-science analysts.

The evidence is conflicting. We do not have sufficient knowledge to predict with any great accuracy what our future skill requirements will be, although considerable research is now under way in an effort to provide better reference points. However, imminent disaster is not around the corner. If one reflects for a moment on the many workers whose jobs are unlikely to be automated in the foreseeable future—baseball players, counter clerks in hamburger stands, gas-station attendants, motelkeepers, to name a few —the outlook is not as bleak as sometimes pictured.

A great many other occupations, and new ones not yet dreamt of, should be added to the list. Another hopeful note can be sounded if we recall the discussion of wages, employment, and productivity in the previous chapter. Improved machinery increases the productivity of the labor that remains on the job and this, in turn, permits the employer to pay higher wages or sell at lower prices, and adds to aggregate demand. As people's real incomes rise, they spend relatively more on services and less on goods. They want more and better medical care, education, recreational and vacation facilities, housing. Productivity in the service industries is rising less rapidly than in manufacturing, and is much less advanced along the automation road. This is a major factor in producing the great expansion in the white-collar labor force that we noted at the outset of this volume.

Though alarmist fears of tremendous automation unemployment may be exaggerated, it would be wrong to dismiss the whole matter as something that will correct itself in the long run, and to conclude that nothing need be done about it. In spite of a substantial population increase, there has been a decline since the war in employment in such consumer-goods industries as food processing, textiles, petroleum products, and leather goods. Employment has also fallen in lumber, basic iron and steel, and automobiles. Insurance, banking, and warehousing have witnessed considerable progress in electronic data processing and control, but in this sector there has been no serious displacement of personnel as yet, though the rate of new hiring has slowed. The federal government was using 1326 electronic computers in 1963, and expects to have 2150 by 1966. About 60,000 persons are employed in the operation of these machines, but many jobs that would have been created have not materialized in consequence of their introduction. There is a net loss.

Perhaps in time there will be new employment opportunities, but in the meantime, thousands of men and women will find that their skills are obsolete and that their occupations have vanished. It is no solace to an unemployed musician who has been made redundant by modern sound recording that there are more jobs available in the technical side of record production. Few believe that technological progress can or should be stopped, but it is the obligation of a society which reaps the benefits of cheaper products to provide compensation and assistance to those upon whom the costs of change fall most heavily.

An average unemployment rate of 4 percent is frequently cited as the lowest that is consistent with a stable economy in the United States. The Council of Economic Advisers terms this an "interim target," but others go further and warn that anything lower would inevitably lead to inflation.

Much of the current reasoning is based on the work of A. W. Phillips, a British economist who conducted a statistical investigation into the relationship between wage changes and unemployment in Great Britain between 1861 and 1957. Phillips concluded that if unemployment stood at 5 percent, money wages remained stable; but that when unemployment fell to 2½ percent, money wages rose between 2 and 3 percent a year.

Phillips' statistics and his methodology have come in for severe criticism. Other analyses of the British experience have not yielded nearly such conclusive results. Attempts to find similar relationships for the United States have not been successful for recent years, and only partly so for earlier periods. It has been pointed out that profits, business expectations, and industrial concentration may yield equally good results in explaining wage changes. Most important of all, the observed relationships between wages and unemployment are not sufficiently precise to permit firm policy conclusions to be drawn from them.

Nevertheless, the idea continues to attract attention. Two eminent American economists, Paul Samuelson and Robert Solow, have stated their belief that under current conditions in the United States unemployment would have to be as high as 5–6 percent to prevent wages from rising by more than 2½ percent a year (this is about the long-run annual growth in productivity), while a 3 percent unemployment rate would result in prices rising on the order of 4–5 percent a year as a result of wage increases. They point out, however, that changes in labor-market institutions could result in modification of the suggested relationship between wages and unemployment.

We have already pointed out in the chapter dealing with trade unionism that labor leaders are less likely to demand substantial wage increases when a good many workers are idle than when labor is scarce. Employers are less apt to bid wages up when a pool of unemployed workers from which they can hire is available. But this is not at all the same thing as the assertion that there exists a fixed, predictable relationship between wages or prices and unemployment, so that if we lower unemployment to rate *x*, we can confidently expect wages or prices to rise at rate *y*.

It is instructive to examine the experience of nations other than the United States in this respect. The relevant

data are shown in the table on p. 121, from which it appears
that in general terms, low unemployment and some price
inflation went hand in hand. However, the relationships
shown are by no means precise; for example, Belgium had
a much higher rate of unemployment than the United
States and still experienced some price rise, while Germany managed to contain price inflation despite relatively
low unemployment.

Great caution must be exercised in drawing inferences
from simple comparisons of this nature. Nations differ in
many respects, and their economies operate in very diverse
ways. All that one can say is that several advanced nations, Great Britain, Sweden, and Germany among them,
were able to maintain low unemployment levels without
running into politically impossible degrees of price inflation. One cannot predict from these data how much inflation the United States would have experienced at, say,
British levels of unemployment, but the experience of
Western Europe at least suggests that, contrary to the
Samuelson-Solow predictions, the trade-off between unemployment and price change may be well within the bounds
of acceptability.

Professor Stanley Lebergott, a prominent student of
American unemployment, has proposed that a maximum
of 3.5 percent unemployment be set as a national policy
goal. With respect to the possible effect on prices, he says:
"American experience suggests that within likely peace-
time unemployment ranges the conflict is not as great as
might appear. Recent studies indicate that postwar wage
changes are largely accounted for by factors other than the
unemployment rate."[*]

My own reaction is that this goal is too modest, if anything. There is no reason why we should not aim at a level
consonant with the postwar experience of the major European nations. One argument often advanced against our
ever being able to achieve, say, a 2 percent unemployment

* Stanley Lebergott, *Men Without Work*, 1964.

UNEMPLOYMENT AND COST OF LIVING IN WESTERN
EUROPE AND THE UNITED STATES, 1953–1961

	Average Annual Unemployment (as a percentage of the labor force)		Percent Increase in Cost of Living	
	1953–1961	1956–1961	1953–1961	1956–1961
France	1.1	0.9	38	34
Netherlands	1.6	1.4	23	14
Great Britain	1.6	1.7	25	12
Sweden	2.1	1.8	28	17
Germany	3.9	2.5	14	10
United States	5.1	5.4	12	10
Italy	6.7[a]	6.2	18	8
Belgium	8.3	7.4	11	7

[a] 1954–1961.
SOURCE: United Nations, *Compendium of Social Statistics,* 1963.

rate is that our economy is so diverse and dynamic as to
require more labor mobility, and hence more unemployment. But this is an assertion that has never been proved.
Europe is also experiencing a great deal of labor mobility,
with men and women in large numbers crossing the barriers of nationality and language in search of work. The
question may at least be raised, for example, whether the
difficulty and time lost in moving from New York to Chicago are really greater than in the move from London to
Manchester, from Stuttgart to Hamburg, from Stockholm
to Gothenburg—to say nothing of Naples to Bremen.

The real problem may lie in attitudes rather than in the
character of the economic environment. The late principal
economist of the Organization for Economic Cooperation
and Development, whose job it was to make comparisons
among Western nations, put the matter very aptly:

. . . it is hard to avoid the conclusion that the contrast
between European and American price history from 1956
to 1962 is an accurate index of a contrast in attitudes.

Much has been said in Europe about the importance of price stability. But nowhere,—not even in Germany, supposedly the classic example of inflation neurosis—have countries been prepared in the event to arrest their growth and create unemployment simply in order to stop prices from rising.*

* Jack Downie, in Arthur M. Ross (Ed.), *Unemployment and the American Economy*, 1964.

VIII

The Attack on Unemployment

and Poverty

Before examining what is being proposed, and what is being done, to reduce unemployment, we should consider the concept of poverty, for unemployment and poverty are closely related. The Council of Economic Advisers has proposed as the test of poverty a family income below $3000 a year in 1962 prices, or an income of less than $1500 for individuals living alone.* Using this point of reference, 8.9 million families with 29.2 million people in them, plus 5 million single persons, or 34.2 million people in all, were living in poverty in 1963. The Social Security Administration tells us, on the basis of a somewhat different calculation, that 15 million children, one-fourth of all the children in the nation, were in impoverished families in the same year.

Most readers will not need much in the way of argument

* Family and individual incomes of this magnitude are well above *average* incomes in many parts of the world. However, this does not mitigate the social and individual consequences that flow from having low incomes in the United States. Poverty does not lead to starvation here, but it does lead to disease, crime, and an ill-afforded loss of human capabilities.

to convince them that $3000 a year is a minimum amount indeed for a family to get along on. If $5000 were adopted as a hardly affluent minimum, an additional 32 million people would fall within the relatively deprived group; this is a total of 66 million, about 35 percent of our entire population.

As with unemployment, poverty has certain structural characteristics. About 43 percent of all non-white families were below the $3000 poverty level in 1963 compared with 16 percent of the white families. Forty-eight percent of the families headed by women were living in poverty, in contrast to 20 percent of the families headed by men. Education was a major factor here too. Of the 7 million families headed by persons with less than eight years of elementary education, 44 percent were poverty-stricken, while at the opposite end of the scale, only 5 percent of the 5.3 million families whose head had a college education were in this situation. The most typical poor family is headed by a non-white woman who has not graduated from elementary school.

Poverty is more regionally concentrated than unemployment. The South has the dubious distinction of leading the nation in this respect, with 31 percent of all its families below the $3000 line. Not surprisingly, 60 percent of all its Negro families fell into this category. The Northeast had 13 percent, the West, 15 percent, and the North Central area, 17 percent. Particular trouble spots within these large regions were Appalachia, the Indian communities of the Southwest, and the slum areas of the large Northern cities. Rural areas in general have more than their share of poverty, despite the fact that the farm population has been shrinking due to migration to the cities. Young people are leaving the land for the cities, and the aging population that remains is falling behind in the economic race.

The heads of only 30 percent of the poor families were employed throughout the entire year of 1963. Of the rest, 16 percent were unemployed for part of the year, 14 percent were in and out of the labor force, and 40 percent were not in the labor force at all during the course of the year. The latter group included disabled and retired persons, and women with small children, but also people who were not looking for work because they had despaired of finding any.

The Committee on Education and Labor of the U.S. House of Representatives said in a 1964 report: "Poverty can be traced back to unemployment, underemployment, and low earnings in perhaps half of the families with incomes under $3,000 in 1962." Measures which reduce unemployment will therefore help about half the poor families, but special programs will be required to deal with the rest.

The federal government, following the policy line advanced by the Council of Economic Advisers, has committed itself to the use of fiscal and monetary measures to increase effective demand, hoping in this way to step up employment. The most striking recent examples of this policy were reductions in federal personal income, corporate profits, and excise taxes.

A portion of the tax reduction is saved by the taxpayer, but most of it is spent on goods and services; the additional purchasing power created exceeds the latter amount because of a "multiplier" effect. When one buys a car, for example, demand is created for the services of the auto worker, and he in turn has more money to buy other goods and services, causing a chain of spending which multiplies the effect of the original purchase. It has been estimated that the tax cut multiplier is about two, that is, for each dollar of tax reduction, two dollars of demand are pumped into the system.

If cutting taxes provides the answer to the elimination of unemployment, why not just keep removing them until the interim target of 4 percent, or an even lower figure, is reached? One of the catches is that the added demand may begin to affect prices.* Production is stimulated, business firms begin to order new plant and equipment, and shortages of both consumer and producer goods may begin to appear. As unemployment declines, certain types of labor may become scarce, resulting in a bidding up of wages. When prices start rising, the more cautious governmental advisers, usually associated with the Treasury Department and the Federal Reserve System, will counsel restraint, even at the expense of halting the boom. Those whose eyes are fixed on the elimination of unemployment are likely to argue that prices should be permitted to rise. Whether the brakes should be applied by raising interest rates, increasing bank reserve requirements, raising taxes, or in some other manner, will be decided in the realm of politics, not economics. The Eisenhower administration was inclined to be cautious, while the Kennedy and Johnson administrations have been more venturesome, though it must be added that no real test for them has thus far been posed.

The issue boils down to whether we are willing to risk a measure of price inflation in order to achieve full employment. What we do not know, as should be evident from the previous discussion of the Phillips theory, is the precise trade-off between price change and unemployment. No one wants a Latin American type of galloping inflation in order to achieve a European level of employment. But suppose unemployment could be lowered to 2.5 percent on the basis of a 2 percent annual price rise? Or a 3 percent price rise?

It is not inconceivable that with proper management of the economy, full employment can be attained together with price stability. The experience of the years 1961–

* It also makes more difficult the balancing of the federal budget. Many people find it puzzling that while an *unbalanced* budget may be disastrous for an individual household, a *balanced* federal budget may be equally disastrous for a slack economy, and consequently there is great political pressure to reduce federal spending. This budget neurosis does not exist in Europe, where budget deficits are regarded as a proper and normal means of increasing demand.

1965 is hopeful, though not conclusive. However, an unchanging price level is not necessarily the equivalent of a sound economy. Price stability may be too high a price to pay for substantial unused resources of men and machines.

A second reservation with respect to the efficacy of tax cutting is that this is by no means the only way to stimulate demand. Increased governmental spending, both on the federal and state levels, financed by borrowing, can do the same thing. In fact, the income multiplier effect may be higher than for tax reduction. Expanding public works is an old anti-unemployment remedy, and there is a good deal to be said for it.

There is some warrant on other grounds for arguing that increased government spending is preferable to tax cutting. Many tend to look upon private spending as somehow inherently better than government spending, and a few of the results are that automobiles are outstripping highway capacity, bowling alleys multiply more rapidly than schools, motels proliferate while hospital facilities lag. A sharp step-up in public-supported housing is necessary to arrest the further degeneration of our cities into vast slums. More recreational facilities, an adequate water supply, and better local transportation can only be secured through government, under our present institutions. There is indeed a choice to be made, but all too often it is made on ideological rather than economic grounds.

A favorite trade-union remedy for unemployment is the reduction of working time, in the form of a shorter work day and week, or longer vacations. The long-run trend is in this direction: at the turn of the century, manufacturing employees worked 59 hours a week, on the average. The work week fell to 50 hours by the end of World War I and to 40 hours during the Great Depression. The two decades since World War II have witnessed little change in this respect, however, and we are still on a standard 40-hour week.

Vacation periods have lengthened recently, on the other hand. Many collective agreements grant long-service employees three- and four-week vacations each year. The 1963 steel-industry agreement took a leaf from the teaching profession by stipulating sabbatical leaves for steel workers: after each five years of service, senior steel workers are entitled to thirteen weeks of paid vacation. The annual number of paid holidays has risen.

The argument made for shorter hours is often deceptively simple. According to the calculations of AFL–CIO economists, each hour cut from the work week will create a labor shortage equal to 500,000 jobs. On this basis, a 35-hour work week would take care of the problem of unemployment nicely, with the additional bonus of shorter hours for everyone.

But the AFL–CIO proposes that this be done without reducing weekly take-home pay, which would be tantamount to a general 14 percent hourly increase. The marginal cost of labor to the firm would rise without any compensating increase in marginal productivity (except, perhaps, for a slight increase in working efficiency due to the shorter hours); labor costs would rise per unit of product; and either prices would have to rise, or workers would have to be laid off, or both. What the net result would be is not at all certain; it would depend on such things as the extent of the price rise, the possible development of skilled-labor bottlenecks, and the spur to increased mechanization to replace the more expensive labor. But it is highly unlikely that there would be a smooth absorption of the unemployed to fill the gap left by the cut in hours, with no effects on production and prices.

As the productivity of our economy rises, we can enjoy the extra fruits in higher incomes, greater leisure, or a combination of the two. It is productivity advance that has enabled us to reduce working time by 20 hours a week since 1900, with an accompanying *increase* in living standards. If productivity rises at 3 percent a year, roughly the current rate, we can cut an hour off the working week each year without increasing labor costs, but real income could not then go up. A choice must be made between higher income and greater leisure, and there is some evidence that people prefer the higher income for the present.

The standard work week in the construction industry has been reduced to 35 hours, and even less, in some cities, but actual working time is usually higher. The shorter work week often turns out to be a device for raising pay through an increase in the number of overtime hours worked, not a genuine cut in hours.

Dual jobholding, "moonlighting," is a common phenomenon. The 4 million people known to hold more than one job, and there are probably just as many that we do not know about, average a 52-hour week. Almost 11 million people with one job worked more than 48 hours a week in 1963, half of them either self-employed or doing managerial and professional work.

The major current issue is that of overtime, since we do not seem to be on the verge of a general breakthrough to the 35-hour week. Production workers in manufacturing have been averaging almost 3 hours of overtime a week for the past few years, and many argue that no one should be permitted to put in extra hours while furloughed workers are waiting for jobs. The Secretary of Labor estimated in 1964 that overtime hours worked by persons subject to the Fair Labor Standards Act (those employed in enterprises which engage in interstate commerce) were the equivalent of 1,250,000 full-time jobs.*

The Fair Labor Standards Act requires that a minimum of time and a half must be paid for all hours worked in excess of 40 per week. Many employers find it cheaper to pay these penalty rates than to hire additional employees, because of the expense of hiring and additional fringe-

* As in the case of reduced working hours, however, it does not follow that the elimination of overtime would actually increase employment by this number.

benefit costs. Moreover, overtime opportunities constitute a selling point in keeping the work force satisfied.

It has been proposed by the federal administration that for industries in which employment is sagging, the Fair Labor Standards Act should be amended to require double-time pay for overtime. This would raise the propensity to hire additional workers if more labor were needed, although some employers might still prefer the flexibility of overtime to the difficulties involved in fitting new full-time workers into the production schedule.

The shorter work week is by no means the only way to reduce work time. Extending the years of compulsory schooling is another possibility, and one that would have the additional advantage of raising skill levels. Early retirement is being encouraged under both social security and private pension schemes, but the evidence is not at all conclusive that most people want to retire young. American society has stressed the intrinsic value of work as opposed to leisure, and many might prefer that the retirement age be raised rather than lowered.

Generalization of the sabbatical-leave principle may yet prove to be an attractive and popular method of reducing working time. In many occupations, manual as well as intellectual, skills begin to become obsolete as soon as school is left behind, and in such new industries as electronics and aerospace the rate of obsolescence may be extremely rapid. Half a year or even a year off every seventh year (following the university pattern) would permit re-enrollment in schools or training courses to upgrade skills. Those who are dissatisfied with their present jobs might want to train for new ones. Obviously, this would be a costly procedure, but there would be an economic feedback in terms of the greater working capacities of those who had undergone retraining. Briefer sabbaticals for rest and recreation add to individual well-being, but there is not the same offset to cost.

The idea of sabbatical leaves for all may seem fanciful,

but if anyone who was working during the 1930's reviews his career, he will be prepared for drastic changes in the years to come. The five-day week, paid vacations, and fringe benefits were all but unknown thirty years ago except for a privileged few. While at the moment people seem to prefer goods to leisure, it is likely that working hours will continue to fall. Severe unemployment would give the economy a sharp nudge in that direction, but even at the present level, collective bargaining is beginning to push toward the 35-hour week.

A more buoyant economy would go a long way toward the elimination of unemployment, but it would probably not do the trick by itself. In any dynamic society, old industries die and new ones are born. New machines render old skills obsolete. Whether technological change is more rapid today than in the past is not easy to say with assurance, but the present rate of advance is fast.

Apart from those who are thrown up high and dry by the onrush of new techniques, there are many people who have never had the opportunity to prepare themselves for work in a modern economy. It is increasingly difficult to find jobs for those who cannot read or do simple sums, and who possess no skills. Discrimination does not yield without struggle to a tighter labor market.

The U.S. government has initiated a series of measures designed to supplement the forces of increased demand. They include:

Unemployment compensation. Our state unemployment-compensation laws were enacted during the 1930's as a first line of defense against unemployment. They were never intended to provide more than temporary relief, nor do they. Duration of benefits is generally limited to a maximum period of 26 weeks in any one year, which may be quite adequate when unemployment is low, but becomes less satisfactory when unemployment deepens and people find it more difficult to find new jobs quickly. In 1958 and

1961, benefits had to be extended on a temporary basis in some states beyond the 26-week period, with the assistance of the federal government.

A frequently cited standard for the benefit amount is 50 percent of wages earned prior to unemployment. More, the argument runs, would dull the incentive of the recipient to find work. This standard has no real basis in fact. Private supplementary unemployment-benefit plans which now cover about 2½ million workers and bring benefit payments above 60 percent of previous earnings do not seem to have any discernible effects upon willingness to work. Other countries pay a higher level of benefits than the United States without running into work-incentive problems. However, even 50 percent of previous earnings would be a substantial improvement over the 35–40 percent now paid. The average weekly unemployment check was $35.85 in 1964. If a family had to subsist on this for half a year, after which the right to benefits would be exhausted, it would in all probability fall below the poverty line. A target for unemployment benefits which provides at least the non-poverty minimum does not seem unreasonable.*

Our system of unemployment compensation is due for a long-delayed overhauling. Coverage should be universal; at the present time, only 75 percent of all wage and salary earners are covered, most of those excluded being in government, domestic service, and agriculture. Both the amount and duration of benefits are inadequate. If we want a mobile labor force, we should improve the circumstances of those upon whom the burden of flexibility falls. There is no social justification for imposing poverty upon

* The precise target, in money terms, is not easy to determine, since (1) most people are not unemployed for as long as six months; (2) there is often more than one wage earner to a family; (3) there may be other sources of income. Dependents' allowances, now paid in twelve states, are a good way of adjusting benefits to need. We accept the principle in our income-tax system; why not in unemployment compensation?

people who help contribute to a stable price level by the fact of their unemployment.

Area redevelopment. The first of recent attempts at a positive program aimed at getting the unemployed back to work, instead of merely providing them with financial assistance, was the Area Redevelopment Act of 1961. The purpose of this legislation was to provide jobs in depressed areas by attracting new enterprise and retraining workers to qualify for the jobs thereby created. A special case is represented by the Appalachian program, initiated in 1965, which is to extend help to an area particularly hard hit by the decline of coal mining and the elimination of many small, marginal farms.

The results of area redevelopment have not been encouraging thus far. Established firms have not been able to qualify for the low-interest, long-term loans that the government has been holding out as bait to new enterprise, and most of the money has gone to enterprises with dubious chances of survival. By the end of 1964, the program had obligated $850 million to help finance water-supply projects, sewer-treatment plants, roads, and hospitals, all supposed to make the communities more attractive places to live and work. But a pork-barrel approach to the allocation of funds for these purposes was installed, as the Council of Economic Advisers acknowledged in its 1965 Report: "Designation of too many areas reduces the possibility of providing aid sufficient to break out of the circle of poverty. Aid must be concentrated where it is most needed and where it gives the greatest promise of producing self-sustaining recovery." More than one-third of all the counties in the United States have been put on the list of those eligible for ARA benefits, which has meant spreading the resources far too thinly. The manpower retraining aspects of the program have not been important quantitatively compared with other federal programs.

The basic idea behind area redevelopment is a good

one. Migration of labor out of depressed areas may help to alleviate unemployment, but it can also be quite wasteful. Great amounts of overhead capital are sunk into these areas, and particularly in view of the growing pressure of population in our larger metropolitan centers, it makes good sense from a social point of view to utilize this capital even at the cost of some additional investment. Natural resources no longer constitute the principal rationale for industrial location; much more important is the existence of an adequate and skilled labor force. The federal government hopes to expand the redevelopment program, and it may yet yield significant dividends if administered as a true development scheme rather than a temporary work-relief project.

Manpower training. In the first 2½ years of its operation, the Manpower Act provided training facilities for 320,000 persons, mainly in machine operation, auto repair, and clerical work. Unemployed trainees are paid allowances while enrolled, and the period of training can last as long as a year. About 70 percent of those who have gone through a training program found jobs, most of them in occupations related to the training they received. Particularly encouraging is the fact that over 65 percent of the long-term unemployed who enrolled in the program, some of whom had been jobless for over a year prior to retraining, were placed in employment.

The program is not without its deficiencies. Chief among them is its limited size. During 1964, only 200,000 persons were approved for training. In the same year, there were 973,000 persons unemployed 15 weeks or more, of whom 482,000 were unemployed for over half a year. There has been too heavy reliance on formal programs in educational institutions, and not enough on the cheaper alternative of on-the-job training. Older workers and the undereducated have not been reached in large numbers, the former because of inhibitions against returning to the classroom, the latter because they could not reasonably be expected to meet minimum hiring standards. About 22 percent of our labor force consists of persons with only an elementary-school education (about 5 percent, or 3.5 million, have less than five years of schooling), whereas high-school graduation is commonly required for skilled and semi-skilled trades. We have scarcely begun to tackle the problem of general education for adults who must learn the basic skills of literacy and arithmetic before they can benefit from more advanced training.

For all its faults, the Manpower Act is a milestone in the acknowledgment of social responsibility for the alleviation of structural unemployment. Prior to the enactment of the law, the prevailing philosophy was that individual initiative provided sufficient incentive for the acquisition of skills necessary for a successful career in the present-day economy. Temporary palliatives in the form of unemployment compensation and outright charity would take care of those who were readjusting themselves to economic change. Congress has now finally recognized that because of insufficient opportunity as children, lack of education and knowledge, or sweeping technological advance, millions of people find themselves outside the mainstream of American life, condemned to marginal employment, low wages, and unstable tenure of work. In an otherwise matter-of-fact appraisal of the program, the government made the following observation:

> Most trainees . . . are enthusiastic about their training, particularly those enrolled in projects for the hard-core unemployed. Department of Labor staff members frequently have witnessed a metamorphosis in such trainees' attitudes as the ultimate prospect of employment restores hope, self-respect, and self-confidence and erases cynicism and bitterness.*

The anti-poverty program. Unemployment and poverty overlap, but they do not coincide completely. Some people

* *Manpower Report of the President,* 1965, p. 137.

cannot work because of family responsibilities or physical handicaps. Others may feel that it is futile to look for jobs, young people in minority groups being particularly heavily represented in this category. The Economic Opportunity Act of 1964 is designed to take over where the Manpower Training Act ends.

The new program is just getting under way, and it will be some time before any evaluation of its results is possible. There are to be Job Corps camps with an initial capacity of 25,000 young people patterned after the Civilian Conservation Corps of thirty years ago, where the main emphasis will be on forest conservation work. Whether at the same time it is going to be feasible to develop attitudes and skills that will be useful upon return to the city is the big question. An additional 175,000 young men and women will be enrolled in a Neighborhood Youth Corps where they will live at home and work on projects for non-profit organizations and government agencies. Here, a major problem may well be the fear on the part of trade unions that work which would otherwise be performed at regular rates of pay will be done at cut-rate wages by the trainees. It was this same consideration that limited the effectiveness of the New Deal's WPA program.

A third facet of the program will provide part-time employment for about 100,000 needy college students. A fourth so-called Work Experience Program is aimed at unemployed heads of families now on the welfare rolls who lack the education, skills, and other capacities necessary for productive work. They will receive job training, though in view of the basic handicaps with which they start, it is not at all clear what this is to be. Closely allied is an adult literacy program, expected to reach 70,000 persons a year, while a Community Action Program is designed to help local communities plan the elimination of poverty by providing job counseling, pre-school preparation, and similar social services. The funds provided to finance all of these programs are substantial: more than $750 million for 1965, and $1½ billion the following year.

The Economic Opportunity Act has been attacked, on the one hand, as grossly inadequate to the task at hand, and on the other as a vast giveaway of federal funds to no good purpose. It is in fact an imaginative program, necessarily multi-pronged because of the structural diversity of the unemployment and poverty problem it is designed to solve. It marks the beginning of a long-overdue national campaign to eliminate poverty in the United States. If the initial results are encouraging, it will undoubtedly be expanded. What seemed utopian a few years ago may yet become a reality.

Our ideas about the inevitability of unemployment and poverty have undergone startling changes within a short period of time. There are still those who hold to the belief that unemployment can be cured by a little judicious wage cutting, but they have lost all influence on national policy. The need for a two-front attack has become widely accepted: through an increase in the demand for goods and services, and through a series of special governmental measures aimed at helping the members of disadvantaged groups.

But we are just at the beginning, not at the end, of what may turn out to be a long journey. The new programs are experimental and affect only a minority of the unemployed and the poverty-stricken. Many employed persons are neither living in affluence nor occupied in tasks which begin to give full scope to their abilities. The problems posed by automation and other forms of technological change are all too evident. The United States needs a positive employment policy, as well as unemployment and poverty programs.

Some of the ingredients of such an approach can be perceived by examining the experience of Sweden, a nation justly regarded as a social laboratory for the West, which has pioneered a so-called "active labor market policy." Part of this is a continuation of a public-works program which reduced the impact of the Great Depression in Sweden even before the Keynesian revolution in economic policy affected the rest of the Western world. What is new is meticulous government attention to the operation of the labor market and vigorous efforts to make it function more effectively.

A first necessary condition is good information about employment opportunities. The Swedish Labor Market Board, through its local offices, receives advance notice of layoffs from employers, and virtually all actual vacancies are listed with it. About 80 percent of new placements are made through the state employment offices, compared with about 15 percent in the United States. Our federal-state employment service normally receives notification of only the less desirable jobs, and it does not serve as an effective job clearing center.

A major weapon in the Swedish employment policy arsenal is the promotion of geographical mobility. Unemployed workers in areas where industrial expansion is not feasible are encouraged to move out by payment of travel expenses; settling-in allowances; payments to their families for periods up to nine months, if they cannot find adequate housing immediately; and moving expenses.* These costs are offset in part by the saving of unemployment and welfare benefits which would have been paid had the unemployed remained in their old homes, so that even from a purely economic point of view the policy has much to commend it.

Parenthetically, it may be noted that many employed

* The first tentative step in the direction of a comparable policy in the United States was taken in 1964, when the Department of Labor initiated several pilot projects under the Manpower Act. Financial assistance to workers who desire to relocate will be limited to grants of 50 percent of moving expenses, or loans up to 100 percent.

persons in the United States receive financial aid to facilitate their moving: this is quite common among corporate managerial personnel. A psychology which regards this as perfectly fitting and proper, and at the same time condemns similar assistance to the much needier unemployed, is difficult to understand.

A third aspect of Swedish policy is an elaborate system of training and retraining programs which can accommodate 1 percent of the entire labor force a year. Particular attention has been paid to training the physically handicapped. Some Swedish economists have urged that paid retraining programs be open to any employed worker who would like to change his occupation, but this has not yet become government policy.

Sweden has not hesitated to use fiscal and monetary policy to maintain a level of effective demand adequate to keep the general unemployment level very low. Its systems of unemployment compensation and old age pensions are considerably more liberal than those of the United States. A national health plan provides a high level of medical care. Public housing has long been a model for the world. As a result, it may fairly be said that poverty no longer exists in Sweden—or in the neighboring Scandinavian countries, Denmark and Norway, for similar reasons.

The Scandinavian countries are small in area, racially homogeneous, without many of the social problems that beset a large nation like the United States. On the other hand, they do not have the wealth of the United States. While it is difficult to be precise about international income comparisons, per capita income in the United States probably exceeds that of Sweden by one-third to one-quarter, with an even greater disparity in the cases of Denmark and Norway.

Neither Sweden nor any other country can provide a complete blueprint for the United States. The Swedish experience has been described only to point up the fact that poverty and unemployment are not inevitable in a modern, rapidly growing, industrial society. The United States possesses the physical and financial resources to provide every one of its citizens with a decent job, but our economic institutions have not been flexible enough to enable us to reach this goal. This can be traced back ultimately to attitudes toward the appropriate role of government in economic life. There are indications that these attitudes are undergoing a fundamental change; certainly the newly initiated federal programs would have been regarded as dangerously radical not long ago. If we persist in these endeavors, and do not hesitate to experiment, most of us may live to enjoy a society free from the degradations of involuntary unemployment and poverty.

Bibliography

Trade Unionism

The best short history of trade unionism in the United States, which also has the advantage of being up to date, is Philip Taft, *Organized Labor in American History* (New York: Harper & Row, 1964). A great deal of information about the internal organization and operation of trade unions is to be found in William Leiserson, *American Trade Union Democracy* (New York: Columbia University Press, 1959).

Collective Bargaining

The major issues of collective bargaining are delineated in great detail in a monumental study by Sumner H. Slichter, James J. Healy, and E. Robert Livernash, entitled *The Impact of Collective Bargaining on Management* (Washington, D.C.: Brookings Institution, 1960). There is an interesting collection of essays on current problems of collective bargaining in Arnold R. Weber (ed.), *The Structure of Collective Bargaining* (New York: Free Press of Glencoe, 1961).

Wage and Employment Theory

The reader would do well to start with the classic study of John R. Hicks, *The Theory of Wages* (New York: Macmillan, 1932). The effects of unionism are considered in another classic, John T. Dunlop, *Wage Determination Under Trade Unions* (New York: Macmillan, 1944).

The Labor Force and Unemployment

The outstanding historical study in this area is Stanley Lebergott, *Manpower in Economic Growth* (New York: McGraw-Hill, 1964). The annual *Manpower Report of the President*, beginning in 1963, contains a vast amount of valuable statistical information about the composition of the labor force, and highlights current problems. The definitive recent treatment of measurement was prepared by the President's Committee to Appraise Employment and Unemployment Statistics, *Measuring Employment and Unemployment* (Washington, D.C.: U.S. Government Printing Office, 1962).

Current Policy Issues

A useful volume quoted in the text is Organization for European Economic Cooperation, *The Problem of Rising Prices* (1961). A good statement of both the theoretical and practical issues is International Labour Office, *Employment and Economic Growth* (1964). *The Annual Report of the Council of Economic Advisers* constitutes an authoritative statement of the position of the United States government on many of the basic issues discussed in this book.

ACKNOWLEDGMENTS

Professor Melvin W. Reder of Stanford University was kind enough to read a first draft of this volume with his usual meticulous care. His observations were trenchant and his advice good, as anyone familiar with his writings would expect. Mr. Peter L. Bernstein, whose *Primer on Money, Banking, and Gold* set a very high standard for me to follow, let me have the benefit of his critical judgment on many points. The task of writing was greatly lightened by the encouragement of my wife, Dr. Marjorie S. Galenson.

The book contains many controversial views, so that it is particularly important for me to accept full personal responsibility for all errors of commission and omission.

Index

ABOUT THE AUTHOR

WALTER GALENSON is a graduate of Columbia University, from which he received the degrees of A.B. and Ph.D. After wartime service with the Office of Strategic Services, and a stint in the United States Foreign Service, during which he was labor attaché in Oslo and Copenhagen, he became assistant professor of economics at Harvard University, where he remained for five years. Since 1951 he has been professor of economics at the University of California, Berkeley. Dr. Galenson has served as arbitrator in many labor disputes, and is a consultant to the International Labour Office in Geneva. He has been a Fellow of the American Philosophical Society, a Fulbright Fellow to Norway, and a Guggenheim Fellow. He is currently Director of Research for the Committee on the Economy of China of the Social Science Research Council.

Dr. Galenson is the author of the following books: *Rival Unionism in the United States* (1940); *Labor in Norway* (1949); *The Danish System of Labor Relations* (1951); *Labor Productivity in Soviet and American Industry* (1955); *The CIO Challenge to the AFL* (1960); *Trade Union Democracy in Western Europe* (1961); and *The Quality of Labor and Its Impact on Economic Development,* with Graham Pyatt (1964). He is the editor of *Comparative Labor Movements* (1952); *Labor and Economic Development* (1959); *Labor and Trade Unionism* (1960); *Labor in Developing Economies* (1962); and a series of books on American trade-union government published in 1962. He has written twenty-five articles in various scholarly journals.